THE CHARGE IN THE GLOBAL MEMBRANE

By B.W. Powe

Street Art Photos by Marshall Soules

NeoPoiesisPress.com

NeoPoiesis Press, LLC

2775 Harbor Ave SW, Suite D, Seattle, WA
Info@NeoPoiesisPress.com
NeoPoiesisPress.com

B.W. Powe – The Charge in the Global Membrane
ISBN 978-0-9975021-8-3 (paperback: alk. paper)
1. Non-Fiction. I. B.W. Powe. II. Marshall Soules. III. The Charge in the Global Membrane.

Library of Congress Control Number: 2018957221

First Edition

Cover photograph: Marshall Soules
Cover, design, and typography: Richard Prevost

Printed in the United States of America

For

Elena Teresa Sánchez-Powe

For

Donna, Tonya and Sadie

Epigraph 1

" To   Situations

New

The effort

to comprise

it

is   all   the

Soul can do,

+ Exhibition —

Comprehension

+   of Comprising"

Emily Dickinson, *Envelope Poems*

BREAKING the NEW

Updating

We're In the Now Alert

Bulletins

On Opening Time and Closing Time, Generations of Electricity, Emerging World Consciousness and Light-Dark Energies, the Donald Trump Phenomenon and the Spectacle of His Election, the Threat of Nationalist Movements and Separatism, Refugees, Pilgrimages of the Soul, Teilhard de Chardin's Noosphere and Gaia, Identity Crises, Empathic Conditions and Conflicts in Sensibility, Media Wars, Clicks, A-literacy and ESP Literacy, Dark Posts and Trolls, Nervousness and Shock, Shattering Instants of New Vision and the Sparks of New Myths, Paranoia and Conspiracy Cults, Silence Breaking, Wave-Free Zones and Tiny Houses, Bob Dylan, Leonard Cohen, Patti Smith, David Bowie, Joni Mitchell's "Woodstock," Net-gens and the iBrain, Sex-sites and Eros, Transformers (the movies), Fire, and the Expanding and Contracting of the Global Heartbeat

Here's /

a seizing of moments /

a venturing into the vibrations /

a poetry collage essay / a journal diary /

a gathering of aphorisms /

a thought experiment that's an attempt /

to put my finger /

on /

the pulse /

the passion /

Again / journeying on the waves / cycling back /

into the current /

Yes / I admit /

to following my fascinations / my obsessions /

"Within a Moment, a Pulsation of the Artery"

William Blake, *Milton*

"Recycling is a key to media ecology"

Anonymous Post

Hey / wait / I hear your voice saying /

this sounds /

weird /

Look at your home fuse-box /

Symbols / codes /

Re / presenting the Invisible /

Flux /

The voltage /

gripping us /

deeper /

into /

its fields /

Yes / it's strange /

much stranger /

than we know or realize /

Are there words /

for this / momentum? /

If all paths / are /

teeming /

then /

what's going /

on? /

Diary of the Charge

March 1st 2017 (Ash Wednesday)

In my satellite-town on the edge of Toronto: late-night hours alone at my desk. I'm taken up by intuitions. When I'm receptive to data migrations. When possessions come. Screen, paper: vibrant spaces blank pages. Crossings, weavings. Switching on until I'm not alone. Multitudes are here. Light, dark energies. Sensational links invite me.

I'm noting...

We continue to experience the charge in the global membrane

... by this I mean immersion. Instantaneousness. Being now... here. Inside electrifying technological environments. All the puns, the associations, in the word "charge" implied.

The ghosts of Marshall McLuhan and Simone Weil haunt my words. McLuhan was the first to fully realize that we're wired up, inside borderless, transnational, immediate, entangling, speeding, here-there-everywhere-now states, in an always intensifying, mutable milieu. Weil said, "Every separation is a link." This crucial theologian and her questions about love and grace, being near to and yet far from the Spirit, waiting for our soul's urgings, for compassion and the communion of being... She engaged our hunger for illusion-delusion, cleansing her senses by ascetic practice, living so bare that she awakened to presence, the potential of vision...

March 8th (International Women's Day)

Deep into night again. My home almost quiet. I should sleep, but I can't. In our bedroom my wife rests peacefully. I get up and return to my work room. Taking out paper: opening my PC. Pen, keyboard. Our house stirs through the vents. Sites on my screen multiply like cells. And I'm writing things down, trying to find pathways to truly perceive...

This is Genesis in overdrive

Once there was the Earth... through communication technologies the Earth became the global village... with the advent of satellites, the village became the Cosmopolis, and it became the global theatre... then PCs and handheld devices, the rule of screens and smartphones: vistas of mobility, instant messaging...

What's the background of these recognitions? The books on my desk: Richard Maurice Bucke's Cosmic Consciousness, Harold Innis's "Minerva's Owl", Simone Weil's Gravity and Grace and The Iliad, or the Poem of Force, Pierre Teilhard de Chardin's The Future of Man, Elizabeth Sewell's The Orphic Voice, Norman O. Brown's Closing Time and McLuhan's The Book of Probes. But these origins are not the point, because the charging of our lives and environments reveals the communal experience of thought and perception, of pulse and light.

In the crucible of this experience we find consciousness expanded, sensibilities stretched. We ravel the threads, the wirings that are conduits for streaming the rush and overflow of transmissions.

March 12th (Daylight Savings: the clocks change)

Early morning. Downloading waves, letting streams guide me again. I make more notes, a shorthand chronology for our hyper-evolutionary state, the wonder and trauma of the wirings:

The first brightened cities
(Gaslight realms, telegraph wires like veins and nerve-end ganglia... 1890s-1910)

Becoming village
(Telephone, radio, cinema, TV... 1920s-late 50s)

Absorbed into theatre
(TV... 60s-90s)

Absorbed into satellite Wi-fi networks
(Home computer... 90s-2000s)

Becoming membrane-cell
(Embracing the above... 2000s+)

Becoming hyper-cellular, Nature and electronica, essentials now merging

in the renewing élan vital, more of the light and pulse of information

These incarnations, prone to being junked, inform the heart of digital consciousness, the heartbeat of linking souls. Weil said, "Who can say what it costs it [the soul], moment by moment to accommodate itself to this residence, how much writhing and bending, folding and pleating, are required of it?"

March 20th (first day of Spring)

In the early morning: writing quickly. Shaking out of sleep and into the currents...

I've adapted the global membrane phrase from what Teilhard de Chardin called the Noosphere in his prophetic <u>The Future of Man</u>. What is the Noosphere? The subliminal layering of externalized thought and emotions around our planet, in our era of exhilarations and depressions, where sensibilities are fine-tuned to acute awareness and responsiveness, and where fear and reaction agitate and haunt the on-line. It is consciousness in a sublime evolutionary phase of extension and embrace, our moods and expressions surrounding the Earth.

The charge carries the sparks of the second Creation, the second Big Bang: the firing-up of technological expansion through electrification and the resultant accelerating streams and impulses of data-energy.

April 9th (Palm Sunday)

Early evening. I make tea. I sit down with my notepad. Making time. Pulling in associations from my imagination.

I want to call this day Psalm Sunday, the time when we could sing and praise. But I'm not very good at singing. And praising must come later...

Now I obsess over the currents' sway, the light-pulse that shapes our experience. It's emerged from individual depths—our technological facility (how fast we've changed our culture and politics)—to depths that flood and run around our lives in oceanic gusts and tides, overwhelming our frames of reference, creating fresh inspirations and polarizing manias, exhilarations and nervous disorders. This experience of immersion and sensitivity is dissolving identities, spawning personal and spiritual crises, and crises of power and finance, while we evolve in the collective jolting of existence. And when we're inundated with on-line images and communal pressures and reactions, we scan the digital inscriptions on firewalls and data-webs to comprehend what's discharging through us.

Still, is it possible to understand this present? Can anyone truly see what's in front of us?

There's a surcharge for our immersions... Chaos and ecstasies... Being possessed by the flux...

April 13th (Maundy Thursday)

I'm up all night, reading *The Way of the White Clouds*... I took this well-known journey book down from my shelf. Turning to passages I remember were quoted by others... And I find... a line to set beside my PC.... Like a talisman...

"Do we really know what electricity is?" asks Lama Anagarika Govinda.

I've tangled with this question for most of my life. I want to write about other things and yet I can't get away from it. Why can't I let it be? Why are my thoughts at its mercy? This beaten path that's never truly beaten.

Lama Govinda writes: "By knowing the laws according to which it [electricity] acts and by making use of them we still do not know the origin or the real nature of this force, which ultimately may be the very source of life, light, and consciousness, the divine power and mover of all that exists... We certainly have no reason to look down upon the animistic beliefs of primitive man, which only express what the poets of all times have felt: that nature is not a dead mechanism, but vibrant with life, with the same life that becomes vocal in our thoughts and emotions."

What are the laws of electricity? I'm disturbed by our immersions in part because electricity may be a source of light and life. Govinda suggests it is. And if energy carries aspects of Spirit and consciousness, then is that why we're embroiled in crises of awareness? Electricity can bring inspirations; also—shock.

April 15ᵗʰ (a day of rest for some cultures)

At my desk. Night thoughts turn into morning meditations. Silence: stillness. I need rest to give me time to be more receptive, yielding...

Saturday alone with a cup of tea, thinking about my notes, these premises. The ramping up begins again:

The global membrane is the result of the advancing metamorphoses, amplified by electronic technology which offers the lighting up the Earth into an artifact (what we contemplate) and a thought-feeling presence (which is our element). This hyper-evolution is both biological—life expectancy has doubled in a century—and sensory-psychic— we're webbed into complexity, sensation, information, imagination, emotion and soul-making.

And poetry, stories? Pivotal ways of understanding the speed-currents of the digital seas...

I acknowledge consequences of the messaging intensity: I'm writing faster, responding rapidly, sometimes repeating myself, with little time for fastidious revision...

April 17ᵗʰ (Easter Monday)

A day when I should be meditating and contemplating. Instead I'm here with my notepad.

In the afternoon. Opening my screen. Disturbing the dust on keys. Venturing onto the web. Keying into...

... the communications' envelope, the atmosphere of circuiting emissions and vibrations. We've added a sphere of communications to the material sphere: human supra-consciousness and feelings now sense-surround Nature.

Our engagements with the dynamic thought-emotion formation are organic (cellular), psychic, political, cultural, artistic-poetic, social, passionate and sexual (erotic). Energy streaming into sites (hot spots), broadband connectives, transmission-receptions and the instantaneous communion of worldwide effects—these are our current-fields of Mystery.

A new form of world consciousness arises: the iBrain, Net-gens... Subject to lightning-fast transformations that galvanize wounded rifts, suppressed emotions, creeping barbarism, intolerance, taints of hatred, and at the same time empathy and sorrow, cries for kinship and love, it seems we're experiencing an intricate thought, an inextricable feeling, and the angry bristling and the warm embrace are two sides of the experience...

Is instantaneousness the sharpest effect of our sensational engulfment? "Are you experienced?" Jimi Hendrix sang over guitars and drums played backwards in his 1967 recording. Yes, we say: "We are; we must be."

April 22nd (Earth Day: we're to dim our lights, be for a few hours less dependent on power-grids; remembering our planet, its grounding beneath the networks. But the perpetual auroras of Toronto radiate undiminished.)

I read and write... with only a single lamplight...

... into the evening...

... The streets in my small town becoming quieter.

Slowing down, reflecting on...

Lama Govinda's pages. I sit with them, sipping my tea, tracing his quest for truths. He describes treks through valleys, mountain passes. His need to comprehend. The encouragement to see that we're transformed by every dimension of existence, whether material, artistic, technological, spiritual...

He writes: "Our consciousness is sensitive to atmospheric pressure and that with increasing 'heaviness'... our consciousness descends into the deepest layers of our mind into our subconsciousness... The greater the pressure the farther we go back."

I stop there, knowing I'm absorbing Govinda's words into my descriptions of evolving world consciousness. Psychic atmospheric pressures, the hyper-intensity of data-spin, fast-forward us into a sensitivity and vulnerability to each other and to the supra-consciousness that the communications' sphere boosts. The greater the pressures of sensation, the farther ahead we leap. The greater the pressures, the more we often react against them.

Natural and technological environmental crises change being

The excess of experience creates evolutionary distress and the promise of greater transfigurations. These intuitions shake us, and lift us.

May 14th (Mother's Day)

I listen to the hum in my home, considering the nature of electricity, its adrenalin and anxiety channels, its omnipresence. Is it caressing, sensual flow—female—and surging, aggressive—male? Do these clichés hold truth? The flux gathering us into waves so that we beat on into the current... the ebb-flow that's chameleon and spark... The presence generating intensities: the presence shattering preconceptions.

(The soul of Wisdom in the Book of Proverbs is called she; and Wisdom is one of the founders of the Earth...)

Listen: the volatizing takes us into the speaking digits of our commune, dial tones and call-ups, the beeps of smartphones and wristwatches, white noise in TVs and PCs, the cry of the Earth herself through ecological instabilities, the ringing in your ears that could be something like the fabled music of the spheres—and to other communications: the silences behind things; one that smothers long-ignored wounds, one that is the deepest enigma...

May 27th (Ramadan has begun)

In my workroom I write in the corners of my pages, filling them with scrawls that go up, down, backwards and forwards. In margin-spaces where intuitions and thoughts cluster in designs like notes scribbled on envelopes meant for letters I want to send, I think of who's there, the soul-presence of all who are immersed...

Can anyone keep track of the membrane's transformations?

How much awareness can people handle?

The processing is beyond me, and likely you. The transitions bring vast conflicts. Once we're inside the web-whorl, we discover there's no privacy. Our personal data could be harvested and put up for sale by pollsters and advertisers. Still, we can try: we can pierce through the screens and the clouds together.

June 5th around 7 pm

No entries.

June 5th (near midnight on World Environment Day)

Stream on... Flowing through... Going deeper into digital seas...

The charge in the membrane initiates an opening time, a new consciousness that won't be suppressed. It also triggers a closing time of stunned reactions—stress that brings repressions and polarizations, the need to block the flux. We ask: what is it we're altering? And what's changing us? Are we being moved to the soulful, an undivided heart? What's moving towards us?

And:

Here are manifestations of the charge appearing at the time of this writing. Be aware (beware) that all airings are subject to change.

Present tense, present tensions. We're living out-of-date.

The Donald J. Trump political-entertainment phenomenon is a crucial moment in the worldwide pulse: he embodies crises in the communications' charge, and he channels and symbolizes enraged reactions to its flux. His appearance is a moment of spiritual and moral emergency in the webs of universal sensitivity and impressionable consciousness. Why? How? He takes us close to hyper-evolutionary terror, the destructiveness that tears at us when we fear we're losing a sense of purpose and of selfhood.

All identities are amorphous: they become more so when borders are fluid and homelands turn into unsettled or danger-ous places. When identity is threatened and bruised, violent behaviour and panicked responses can follow. In the refugee migrations we see people fleeing, driven to find new identities, escaping from places in vicious convulsion. They're turning from their heartbreak, impelled to seek paths they hope lead to an opening in a new heartland. These are forced pilgrimages born out of radical political and ecological volatility. But refugees and migrants often find hostility and reaction: barbed-wire barriers and the shout for increased border protections. This is the voice of the closing: I come first. One of the definitions of suppression is a closing down.

21st-century nationalist movements, whether based on ethnicity or economic concerns, are about walling out surges of sensational change. They're destined to form repressive, exclusionary states. Political nationalism has become a pathology which makes virtues out of disintegration and inhumanity to one another. Build a wall, voices clamour: make sure your territory blocks out your neighbours. Disregard the rule of law and constitutions, riled voices declare: be certain that your political stance disregards a pluralism of meanings.

Sometimes nationalist movements claim they merely want to rearrange trade deals. This cloaks the urge towards insularity and grievance with others who are also often deemed to be oppressors: someone, whether black, white, Latino, Muslim, Jewish, Christian, atheist, female, gay, trans, an exile or a refugee, an immigrant from another part of the world or from the same country, on the political left or the right, must be to blame for the challenges of being here, too close in the intricacies of ever-more intimate lives.

Nationalist movements thrive on anger and bitterness. They propel us into abysses of vitriol and retort by demonizing others, calling them an infiltrator, a traitor, an invader, an intolerable liar, an outlier, an interloper, an undesirable foreigner, an illegitimate outcast.

And thus constrictions begin. And so begins the territorial outcry, "This street... my street." And so starts the talk of bloodlines, who's pure in their lineage and who isn't.

And thus the bonds of love and justice are broken. And so wars begin over language use, who speaks for their group. These appear when people demand a nationalist status because they feel their identities are under threat, besieged by waves of transformations (psychic, sensory, cultural, financial) that can't, apparently, be shaped except by closing borders and by narrowing concerns through promoting the harsh, reductive delusions of a separatist regime.

Expressions of nationalist fervour are about preserving set identities at any cost

and about shutting down or retrieving borders in a world that is jumpstarting towards the communion of souls.

By this I mean we are sharing pilgrimages towards understanding and enlightenment, solidarity with the experience of estrangement, humiliation, abandonment, sorrow and suffering. This communion and these pilgrimages incarnate the yearning for justice and generosity, our need to participate in abundance and to spread the wealth, our desire to break free from loneliness and incessant fatigue, our longing for kinship, our fervent attempts to care for people who suffer from razing storms and rampaging killers, the faith that in the communications' spectrum we could be sending-receiving waves that seek what's best in us, our sense that we're at our bravest when we participate in the spirit of trust, empathy, salaam and love.

We go into streets and to sites finding the experiences and the images of hounded, hurt people, and sympathy may stir. The current of compassion may rise—and could keep rising—when people respond to horror and crisis by finding ways to help, to feel a route through blinding disaster towards awakenings: these are signals that the amped current of mania and violence is (or can be) met by our capacity for tempering sensitivity and kindness, reconciliation and mourning.

Let us make a leap in thought and look into the appearances:

Migrants and spiritual pilgrims share this in common: they make desperate journeys. Why desperate? Everything is at stake. Outcasts flee across the globe, often bringing a suffering so intense that they move us with their pulses of grief. Injured souls long to break away from what wounds them. Spiritually avid pilgrims go wandering, craving enlightenment (travelling in their imaginations or on sacred pathways), to be moved towards sympathetic vibrations. Ecstatic souls tend to look for open ground, frontier places to explore (going on the road to find meaning). All are in flight.

Are exoduses and pilgrimages manifestations of the urgent flow and our unmooring in the global membrane-cell? They can be geopolitical (physical) and psychic (emotional)... People painfully participate in forced voyaging, trekking into fate or destiny, leaving the familiar behind, sometimes clinging to their memories of home and roots, often suffering over their longing for restorations of what they knew. People use social media and search engines to de-familiarize, becoming untethered from the ordinary isolation of the day-to-day self, to find newsflashes and images, avid for relations and profiled communities yet sometimes railing against the sense of uprooting, looking to belong to something that's hard to define.

However, refugees—migrants—rarely have a choice in their agonized flight. Pilgrims choose their paths. Yet (I'm trying to grasp this) in vistas of our strange commonality (all is connected—electricity welds together apparent contraries), people cross borders in exoduses of misery and promise, people in front of screens send responses and a part of their consciousness into the ether, their expeditions into the globe a part of the daily mass.

The point is, surely, to find the covenant with journeying, crossing borders into solidarity with one world, the Cosmopolis of souls, the common home of the Spirit.

In these intersections of apprehension, we see a crystallizing of exoduses and pilgrimages that are physical and digital. Vulnerability and anguish can simultaneously come from the influx of people and the excess of data and sensory strain. What unifies this is the uprooting: smash-up and release. These conditions can create empathy and hard feelings. Thus we find the calls for solace and reciprocity (to welcome the streams); the shouting out for punitive or restrictive actions (stop the unlimited roaming); the sense of over-crowding and asphyxiation (voices being choked off); the need for voyaging (to new sites that promise openings or restorations of reassuring relations); the feeling that life is reeling out of control (in turmoil); the sense that we're living at turning points unknown to other times (in perpetual crises); the moments creating the sensation of being overrun and overcome.

Rapidly morphing conditions don't allow for easy adaptations. People are susceptible to crack-ups and breakthroughs in perception, turnovers of anxiety and the heightening of awareness.

The worldwide membrane is more about ripples of sensibility than it is about ideologically determined positions. It induces conflicts between receptivity, forbearance, emphatic imagination, generosity, patience and forgiveness, and callous and stereotyping reactions, suspicion, inhospitable judgment, fear and abusiveness...

... But in moments, on revelatory frequencies, when we tune into the oscillations in the digital seas, recognizing our soul in the membrane's seething mirrors... we find openings and closings occurring in our culture and politics... and these openings and closings existing within each of us... in you and me...

And because we're immersed in waves of effect and response, inside the impulsions of the new, we see:

Isolation and connection: each brings loneliness; each brings the hunger for immersion. The paradox: loneliness and connectivity merge when our locations are everywhere and nowhere in the membrane's worldwide womb. The anxiety of loneliness is strongest when the flux and spin are at their most vital. This is dislocating to the psyche.

The anxiety of loneliness is our deepest form of alienation. It's our given: overcoming, transcending, healing or channelling lonely anxiety is our hope. Anxiety and the desire to staunch the bleeding of fear are usually the first responses to what's tense and raw. These conflicts are not theoretically shaped: they're informed and streamed by the emotions of the instant and the paradoxical immersions of the soul in the borderless impact of energy-fields.

When data saturates our sites, and transformational sites overstress our nerves, resentment and repulsion rise in reaction. Prickled, stirred out of their isolation, people often ask, "Who's taking away our power? ...Who's in control? ...Who's robbing us of our say? ...Who's the enemy? ...Who's slipping over the borders? ...Where is the charge taking us? ...Who's mixing in? ...Who's infiltrating our values?" In the internet undercurrents of customized sites, voices can be gnawed by grievances. Appalled recoiling may turn to loathing and aversion. These attract the dark energies of viciousness and violence.

And yet in complementary tides, in the christening of energy-fields,

there's unprecedented ease with screens and web data. We commune across the globe and across the street. People accustomed to quick texting and multimedia send-receive outside time zones and zip codes, becoming unbounded, thriving with horizons that seem wider than the sky. "Where are you...? *Skype* me..." a Net-gen message runs. People sometimes call Skype the compassion device because it provides conduits for seeing and talking to family and friends.

Net-gens, in their teens and early to mid-twenties, have been accused of having an unwarranted sense of entitled access to the membrane's energies. "The pampered ones... with too much too soon," annoyed critics say. Let's flip this either-or critique and turn it into a perception. Many Net-gens sense the task of deep participation in the charge, which offers a way out of isolation and fragmentation, by grasping how the new whorl is flame and current, an ebb-flux generating journeys and meeting-points, concurrences in the digital seas. Realities (multiple intelligences) are available through portals. Generations inside the inheritance of electricity must teach those who are on its edges. (I want to address the Net-gens directly later.)

... And to the banner-shout of separatism and racial divide, *"This street... my street,"* came the counter-calls of rallies that engaged people of many generations in many cities, *"This is one world, our world... We will not let hate win..."* The countering is the call against the estrangements of lonely fear: it's the charge of meaning (the reversing of magnetic fields), the calling of the mind and heart to those who move across borders and search into the air, who know that the migrations of data and souls are our frontiers.

These are some sensationalized responses to being wired into breaking immediacies, transforming currents...

... All messages travelling faster than carrier pigeons ever could...

*A pause... To make a break in the fourth wall...
Through truly there are no walls in data-stream...*

How has the film of communications altered Nature herself? Note that the internet ecological banner phrase is "How do we make the Earth great again."

[img7]

Conceive of the world breathing. Conceive of the world bruised and breathless. Perceive the air-glow, the diaphanous covering of our atmosphere, sea-blue, white-tinged, what we need to live: this is the image of the Earth that we see in NASA or Google Maps photographs. Consider how the air-glow is beginning to fray and rip, leaving holes. Natural disasters multiply, intensifying in their catastrophic effects. Air pollution in overcrowded cities causes, among other dire afflictions, a painful increase in people's breathing problems.

Media ecology merges with environmental ecology when the twin movements seek common concern for effects on sensibility and the living planet. They're defining points of awareness for a universal humanity, when we're faced with technological and climate change or cataclysm and with how to keep our souls and our world Greening.

The Gaia Hypothesis, or Principle,

was articulated by Lynn Margulis and James Lovelock in papers published in 1968 and 1969, and then developed in conferences Margulis and Lovelock directed in the 1980s and 90s. While controversial, subject to both wholesale acceptance and curt rejection by ecologists and scientists, the hypothesis states that the world is a being. The Earth, our mother, the sea-blue planet, exhales-inhales, creates and remakes, metamorphosing in webs of dynamic interconnection.

Gaia is a shorthand term for chthonic stirring. This is the first layer of our existence: soil and seed, air and water, biological, material, seedling, bacterial. All things are food for one another, in a Eucharist-like exchange. Mothering is muttering: the Earth speaks to us in weather and biology. The analogy we can make is the sound of the heartbeat that the baby hears in the womb. But the great Mother is a changeling. Fecund and desolate, she's a lover and devourer, enwombing, radiant, nurturing and vengeful, savaging, soothing, seductive and withering...

Some critics see Gaia to be more poetic metaphor than scientific paradigm. But let us for our thought-experiment purposes allow the metaphor of the living Earth to coincide with the perception of the amplified electronic membrane...

Here's an astronaut's vision of Gaia. Yuri Gagarin said: "[On]... the first day or so we all pointed to our countries; the third or fourth day we were pointing to our continents; by the last day we were aware of only one Earth."

Now Nature's elements and creatures are on the run from us. The ecology movement emerged from the acute sensitivity that perceives Gaia lashing out in grief and pain, raging punitive moods, communicating with us, or ex-communicating us, in a life-death struggle of seed-renewal and extinction. Gaia is imperilled by abuse and neglect, pollution in all its forms.

The ecstatic waves of Creation are being jarred by the amped waves of the second Creation.

There are auguries of climate turbulence. Look at how climactic stories of catastrophe dominate us: movies and TV dramas, documentaries and nature channels, environmentalist talks and activist protests, warn us that Gaia is convulsed by seismic fluctuations.

Planet tremors topple towers, tidal waves drown beachside villages and resorts, winds smash down crops and buildings, animals flee into remote hills and forests, rivers flood banks and submerge riverside homes, tornados engulf towns, dust gluts streets and clogs machines, power outages black out cities and villages... Crops are scorched into ashes or soaked into inedible lumps... Diseases and fevers spread with no cure, toxicities are passed on through kisses and touch (toxins generate a fear of epidemics and infected flesh)... On TV zombies stomp relentlessly through the dregs of civilizations... Horror tales in movies show possessed houses with ghosts trapped on this plane of things, hovering and howling beneath the floors and above ceiling beams... These stories haunting us because we read about suburban homes making their residents ill with asbestos and chlorine infections... Radioactively amok microwaves wither food into smouldering morsels... Forest fires flume up, menacing park and animal sanctuaries, smoke gagging people in towns and cities far away from the flames... All disclosing corrosion and displacement, how Nature and Super-Nature are altering, sometimes warring with one another...

Again: our awareness of radical sensory change is expanded when we recognize the communications' dimension we've added to the Earth. Call it the thought-emotion sphere, the electroscape merging with Earth's land-and seascapes.

In this passage from his *Literature and the Gods*, philosopher-essayist Roberto Calasso makes plain how our communications' moment has absorbed Gaia:

... another powerful holistic machine is at work,

a machine as big now as the planet itself... this

new entity is radically different from those that came

before. Here for the first time the natural world is

no longer that which surrounds and encloses a

a community, but that which is itself enclosed... This

new and boundless community is governed by rules

based on phantoms and procedures—rules no less

binding than those of ancient communities. Before

such an all-embracing power could establish itself,

a coup d'état had to take place... by which the

analogical pole was gradually supplanted by the

digital pole, the pole of substitution... on which are

based both language itself and the vast network

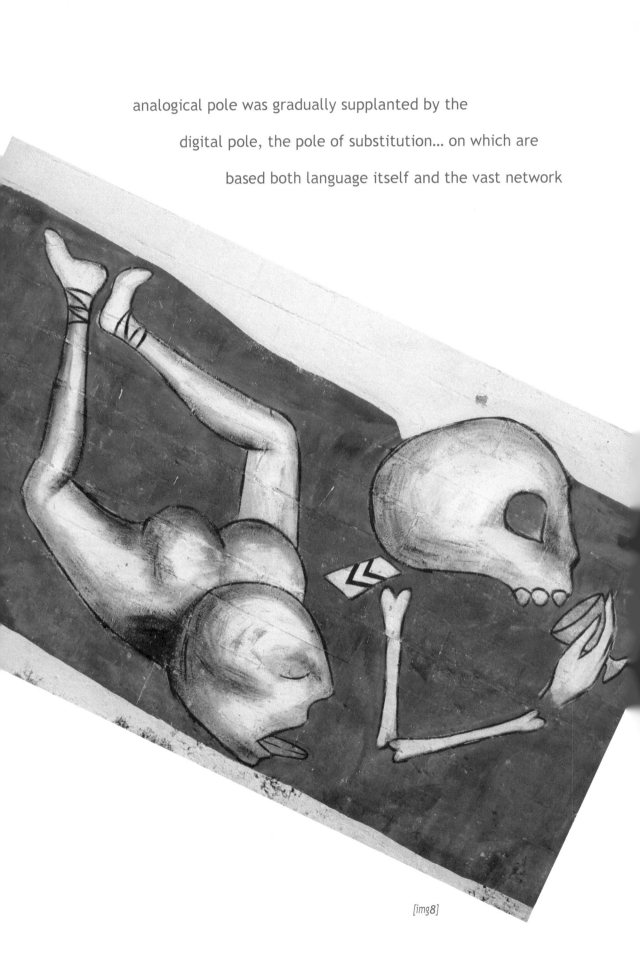

of procedures in which we now live. This

phenomenon [is] at once psychic, economic, social

and logical... Its Zeus is the algorithm. From this

revolution all else follows...

Gaia is the offering of planetary life: we live in
environments that nurture us and devastate us. The Noosphere is
our magnification of the offering. Appropriately, our technological
expressions have names that are biological in origin: cells,
earbuds, sensors, flow and waves. We perceive Gaia through
imaginative, technologized eyes that remake what we see.

Enter this: the communications' sphere, our sublime
invention, is subject to our moods. It's animated and influenced
by stories and ideas, by prayers and petitions, squabbling
and hectoring, reactions and reflections, sacraments and
impoverishments, by the circulation of letters, video-images,
symbols and numbers, by the ecstasies of poetry, the premises of
physics, the crying for love, the presaging of world consciousness...

Whirlwinds in the atmosphere of communiqués emerge
from desperate hunger, praise, mania, lonely humiliation, the
sound of attacks and first responses, projections, cravings, terror
and dreams...

Voices, voices, and images, dramas, everywhere...

Let us look at more manifestations of the Trump crises of spirit and mind.

Trump's call to "Make America Great Again" linked to his climate change denial. It was a tough-line retrieval action: one that wanted to restore the American empire identity of the 19th and mid-20th centuries, and one that tried to refute how our destinies are entwined with technology and the natural environment in a complex Gaia-like dynamism.

Mechanical industrialization and its pollutants are giving way to an information culture where the primary value is Greening. Nature teaches us transformative flow. Rain and underground water sources become rivers: rivers are channelled into hydroelectricity: hydroelectricity feeds technologies. Light filters into satellites, gravity and propulsion curve those crafts around the globe. Signals circumnavigate our planet, possibly passing through it too, alongside what scientists call telluric currents. Nature and Supra-Nature together oxygenate and accelerate motion, resisting stasis.

All identities, ergo, must be provisional. "How very one minute ago," the saying goes... Meaning: the speed-effect ushers in the exigencies and ecstasies of selfhood, pinched and pitched feelings of crowding and exhilaration. We become achingly self-conscious, susceptible in quick-time to upheaval.

Critics called Trump's climate change denial and relentless twittering the last gasp of a spectacular angry paranoia. They've called it the historic revival and assertion of a crude authoritarian impulse in America before an enlightened time comes, or nuclear Armageddon obliterates us. "... in the blink of an eye, the last trump: for the trumpet shall sound..." (Corinthians 15:52). These are exaggerations, of course. Though let's acknowledge that hyperbole and foolhardy remarks are sometimes necessary for us to perceive patterns. Further, we should be careful about thinking that any appearance was or is the last of anything... But if the Trump manifestation became so influential and representative, then what does it mean for the worldwide cell and mind?

[img9]

Crucially, Trump used communications' media in an elemental way. He understood how we're tuned into digital experience. It amplifies the gnawing and itching of sensation and impression, the currents of shock that produce storms of reaction in attentive, eager audiences.

Trump's mastery of Reactive-Insult Currency was on vivid display during the American federal election of 2016. Presidential candidate Hillary Clinton, a private person, a policy wonk, a.k.a. a literate person, couldn't counter the intuitive magic of one so connected to hearsay, "post-facts," conspiracy theories, public retorts that become derisive stand-up routines, seemingly inexplicable reversals in positions and fuming spectacles staged to achieve high populist ratings.

The media theatre can instantly spin into Circus Maximus. Those who understand the magnetized stimuli of the tumultuous carnival thrive in ways that leave others staggered.

Politicians and citizens who opposed Trump vowed to "Go high when others go low," and over many months during the campaign, and then after, participated in reverse abuse, on-line threats, caricaturing (Clinton called her opponents "bigoted deplorables"), airily snobbish dismissals ("there are no ideas in their camp") and even calls by celebrities for assassination. The worldwide membrane processing permeates deeper into our psyches and sensibilities than the infotainments of TV and radio news-briefs. It induces us into its spurring effects, performers and audience alike, fusing ideological divides with emotional drives so that we're all communicants, all supplicants...

Souls among the sensations

our fascinations and rages meld us

into flaming days and nights

[img 10]

From his campaign's blitzing start Trump grasped that tweet-storms incite sensory pressures: the whorl of instability. He knew that the truest rule of capital is pandemonium, the world at economic war: destabilizing deals that only those in-the-know may negotiate.

Capital chafes at the prohibitive boundaries of the law. The rich become richer because they understand capital; therefore, the thinking goes, let them do what they do so that wealth "trickles down." Note the streaming metaphor that capital apologists use.

Hence Trump's rule had to be one that magnified streaks of upheaval. Bankruptcy, market surges and crashes, unemployment, failing medical care, outrageous housing prices, jobs stolen by illegal immigrants, bloated government, skewed trade deals, the nuclear threat from rogue states—these impend. When Trump became President in 2017, his narrow interests became transparent: the financial benefitting of his family (members of his tribe) and his followers (beneficiaries of his franchises and titanic largesse).

Hopeful observers waited to see if Trump would evolve into a cunning Presidential figure—in the line of Washington, Jefferson, Adams, Lincoln, FDR, Eisenhower and Obama. They waited in vain. Officials and family members who work for him had to get smaller to serve him. They humbled themselves like Kafka's tiny creatures who knew they had to squeak and genuflect if they were to survive.

The firings and hirings on Twitter showed malicious caprice. The Twitter feed became legislative fiat. It revealed Trump's true being: a savage media adept who understood the power of inciting his avid audience (his base, and everyone who tuned into the epic) and the addictive fluctuations of spectacle and currency.

Let's reflect on the instantaneous communicating energies of the digital seas.

With over two billion people on Facebook, it's a turbulent ocean unto itself, where nothing is lost in its rush and ripple, the data exhaust trails. More than two-thirds of the population of the planet now live in cities or in towns... People wiring one way or another into the current...

In social media, profiles, stories, impressions and pictures are emitted, floating in the speedy osmosis. These may be skimmed, deleted, stored and re-posted. The processing is unsparing, its unending flash is bedazzling. The shimmer and teeming of the data torrents are the attraction, the spell of clicking in or on. Facebook's escape from categories is a sign of its force. Sparks of mind and spirit have been extended into its sites and waves.

(Fact-checking: I'm not on Facebook. I don't twitter or Instagram. I don't own an iPhone or wear a watch; and I stay away from email for two days a week. Still, the impact of all these is felt everywhere, always.)

Facebook has multiple effects: it's a consequence of hyper-sensitivity, and it instills and abets our reactiveness and impressionability. Twitter-Tumblr-YouTube-Facebook action is about identity, self-expressive, self-promoting, based on blurbs and signs, snapshots and acronym outlines: telegrammed sketches of personality, silhouettes of tastes. One post contains immensities. "Like," "Love," "Laugh," no response at all—these could turn a life towards a public humiliation and an alluring liaison. Users update I.D. status, adding or dropping friends, keeping inside the immersions ("It's complicated"). "Troll emotions" may mean too much emotion and none at all. Posting a "Laugh" could be joyful and derisive at the same time. A radicalization site sometimes leads to recruitment to a terrorist cause. Incessant messaging can decisively alter the moods of political debates. Dark posts barb and afflict us when lies and smears are routinely Uploaded and Shared.

In screen mediations, users share opinions and feelings with invisible crowds that they would never express to a person in private. An implication: the web is without gravity. It's the field where saying anything is permitted because meaning is transient, though subject to harvesting and suspicion. Everything soaked up into the fleeting velocity and amplitude... the waves submerging and whirling people into

Web entanglements

rolling and unrolling

anonymous and discrete

[img11]

Cyberspace is in part technological, in part physical (your hands must touch a keyboard to make it work), in part psychic (your mind merges with unseen impalpable throngs), in part political (the content could be propaganda posted by troll farmers), in part economic (corporations and political movements benefit from people communing on-line), in part a domain of aliases (who's calling you?): algorithms and codes in circulation. Even with filters, advertisements and paid-posts—revealingly called commercial feelers—come seeping in. Petitions to delete and regulating laws appear meaningless in the wake of the high-speed churning...

Data never rests

hacking running

sunrise sunset

When a user takes a breather, he or she must sense how the spinning reels on. People find themselves excluded. Yet people are expected to be reachable at all times. You may choose your images but you can't change how they're received: their effects are magnetizing, whirling. Suddenly un-friended, or stalked, you could find yourself asking, what am I missing? Is someone using my profile? Who's targeting me? Who's harvested my likes and dislikes? Do I have the right to be forgotten?

It's said that Uploading and Sharing can never be an authentic reflection of a person. What we get are mediated perceptions. But if we consider birth, the pangs of love, private thoughts, the difficulty of expressing our sorrow over losing people we love, and communication with God through prayer and ritual, then we must ask ourselves, what isn't mediated? What truly reflects who we are?

Let's see how the charge affects reading, receiving, probing, glancing, riffing, intuiting, leafing through… making associations…

Illiteracy means a person can't read an alphabetic work. Post-literacy means a person nostalgically recalls the act of reading a book or a printed page. A-literacy means a person has no interest in reading a book.

I want to posit a frontier of extra-sensory-perception literacy. Implying: a person could not only read words and sentences but also apprehend and assess the elements and saturations—the runes and cartoons, the propaganda and trolling, in the wilderness of communications where our nerves and minds are being tingled and addressed.

Social media could spell the end of libraries and bookstores… one thing at a time… letters, postcards… longer sentences with complex clauses… metered poetry… and breathing spaces… quiet… But they also call up a lingua adamica, communal and commercial, image-based, a transient poster-board for the shapes and impacts we register in the monetized streaming…

[img12]

Wave patterns sway

back and forth all is doubled, mirrored

rising falling in the digital seas

Everyone who buys a screen and keyboard, an iPhone or tiny earphones, has access to trans-border visions, fanciful scenarios, the wizardry of unfolding picture-grams, internet search engines, tutoring voices in podcasts. Each portal can be a source of leaks, connectives, stimulations, vocal presences. Earphones so small you may not be aware someone is wearing them. Home-screens widened and thinned, images turning ultra HD, 4K, the resolution enhanced. Virtual Reality Glasses engulf us deeper into screen-fields, colour streams searing right into your psyche.

VR extends entries into artificial paradises, expanding alternative realities. **AI** robots work faster than we can, promoting inklings—the goading worry—that they know more than they say or do. The result, we perceive in magnified ways.

Our senses grow accustomed to constant upgrades, the augmenting recreation of our milieus. Sharpened sensations grip us, stimulating and over-stimulating. But we know there's no checking the animations, and we find it almost impossible to look away.

Smartphones obsolete at the moment of purchase... New devices expanding the capacity of ones coming before...

Making selves remaking senses

Awakening to auto-suggestions of impelled evolution

Stare into the fire without insulation

Know your selfie

Aspects of the second Creation

Searing in our hyper-state

*"The new electric environment is a collective poem," McLuhan
said.*

*This means we sample together what poets and visionaries
have perceived and prophesied: all is vital, permeating,
amorphous, shape-shifting, in a stream of shimmering electrons
(atoms): all things radiate, interpenetrate: everything connects
and can be sensed anywhere: time is mercurial: everything
endures in new forms because energy is being constantly
transmuted: the effects of energy will be directly felt and
absorbed through the material fields of technology: matter is
reshaped because of technological manifestations: we struggle
for clarity, definition, form, precision because we know existence
is in flux: our created realms are sites where the Spirit and our
spirits roam, because we know that our rooms and clocks don't
have a radical hold: now we send-receive, screen sites turning
us into hyper-angels and hyper-demons, though truly we're new
mythic creatures, part flesh, part energy-currents, often masked
avatar beings, often released to flit like Shakespeare's Ariel.*

We're so accustomed to our supra-mundane existence in the whorl of amplitude and clicking that we've become unconscious of how arcane it is. Through digital web-memory, we search for errors and obscured backgrounds: we trace ancestries, launching investigations and accusations, weave through invigorating and sometimes dismaying quests for identity—the DNA of stories—amid the spill of images, voices, effects and amazements. Abiding in the ambience, we're magically in touch with enflaming energies, nerve-wracked at times, and yet the transmuting conditions seem routine or banal.

Imagine this Friend Request: *"Do you know Dante, Blake, Emily Brontë, Mary and Percy Shelley, Rimbaud and H.D.? Your friends are asking you to join them..."* Face-the-book... The brand name cunningly encodes facing and the face-to-face moment: the interface of the book and screen with our obsessions with dreams and nightmares, for the crossroads of confrontation and disclosure. Branding is an expression of the need for a purpose. And thus, Facebook screens blaze with our desires: to leave a trace: to book space-time, upload a story, and copy, paste, parody, embellish and revise it.

Does screen magnetism addict us to becoming and to the excitement of extending energy-fields?

...app euphoria comes when a user experiences a trigger and an action brings an immediate reward. iPhone founders call this process "designing minds." On-line reports claim people need interventions—outside interruptions, support groups—to stop paying brittle attention to the intoxications of phenomena. A program for detoxifying data is an app called Forest. You're invited to plant a tree in your mind every time you feel the urge to look at a screen. You're also encouraged to plant a tree in Nature. (Forests are often healing groves in Gaian myths.) The irony: a PC program is available for free to deprogram you.

The adrenalin of access feeds our susceptibility, our vulnerability, to the manifesting thought-emotion. "If it's on Facebook," a maxim states, "then it must be true..." MIT researchers reported in *Science* magazine in 2018 that fake news and hoaxes will spread much faster than real news...

Let's see our mesmerizing and often hooked conditions through a metaphor: the phoenix in our souls seems to be pursuing an arsonist, and the arsonist we've infused into our technologies seems to pursue our phoenix souls. (Metaphor courtesy of Saul Bellow.)

We're malleable beings, our identities subject to igniting influences from many sources, sublime and subliminal, our sensibility shift to available media transporting us into the day-night wonders, the spellbinding, spurring receptivity to light-dark energies...

Suddenly a typo

Covfefe

[img13]

And we begin to contemplate the Adamic possibilities for revealing the structures of revelation.

According to Kabbalah, one misplaced word, a typo, a misplaced piece of punctuation, an unfamiliar syllogism, a chanted syllable or vowel, can take you to another word and then to another underneath. Soon the transcendent intricate dimensions of the world begin to open. Many light-dark energies dance around associations.

But the accidental word, the typo, the lost comma, the half-erased term, the broken sentence, could lead you to being mesmerized by absences and implications... to misunderstanding and anxiety, the alienated stranding in the wilderness of ordeals. A typo could take you to the brink of new meaning and a threat of wider obsessions.

Covfefe

This is what Trump's Twitter feed said on May 30th, 2017. The full tweet said, "Despite the constant negative press covfefe"

The typo or new word concentrated world attention.

Subsequently, newspaper editorials expressed outrage. Baffled media exegetes started offering Talmud-like interpretations. Contributors to Urban Dictionary and Hashtag tried to translate it. How do you pronounce it? Graffiti splashes appeared on walls in Toronto with the word misspelled. It was fodder for Twitter feeds. "That was just fun... But also an official statement... He knows what he meant," said Sean Spicer, then Press Secretary for the White House.

Should we bother with it? Many say, "No."

Still, if we're moving towards the Spirit, into our time, and into what magnetizes us, then its fuel may prove to be part of reshaping psychic energies. We can see how "post fact" means "after eloquence" and "after learning." Let's propose: the tongue of living speech includes blurts and gasps. These are integral forces in the membrane's pulse. Slips and spoofs are part of the Attack and Retreat Rhetoric that often follows on-line posts. "Posting" is integral to the Reactive-Insult Currency. And Blog Rage is another aspect of the trending that some viewers name The Attention Economy.

Was Covfefe a code in the algorithms of clicks? In texting fast reactions dominate. It could have been a cryptogram giving permission to attack people who report on things—the so-called elites who protect intellectual property in the age when copyright has been obsolesced by internet availability. It could mean division, sex, money, force, war. Then again maybe it was a code for sensations we can't articulate yet.

c
o
v
f
e
f
e

Imprint it on a T-shirt to make it emblematic of the spin and flux. Turn it into a PC password. Make a Dada poem out of it. Defuse it by forgetting it...

Still, it was part of the digital texting where the context is more important than the utterance.

Stubbornly, I try to understand it. Defiantly, the word yields nothing obviously semantic. It could be the "Nothing that is not there and the nothing that is," which Wallace Stevens describes in "The Snow Man." But the structures of law, constitutionality, trade arrangements, literary discourse, theoretical protocol and editorial logic must tremble and falter in the wake of what seems a spoof, a blank, a gnome that became viral, an intimation of images and sensational effects to come, because their ground is alphabetic (linguistic).

Eloquence, persuasion, figures of speech, the Ulysses-like capacity for verbal dexterity—these have long been overcome by garbling, the closing down of the ability to write. But silence isn't the result. Silence surrounds and engirdles the word. I find something else happening.

Typos have an illustrious history. James Joyce merrily incorporated errors into the puns of *Ulysses* and *Finnegans Wake*. "The medium is the massage" was a printer's mistake that amused McLuhan, prompting him to use it for the title of the book he intended to call *The Medium Is the Message*. Susan Howe and Anne Carson composed luminous, enigmatic poems out of misreading and typos. The Bible, we know, is riddled with translations of words that are at best speculations on the original meanings.

C o v f e f e

...doesn't seem to be a word of fire or redemption. Yet it carries the branding of the new...

An ending and a beginning...

It's a break into abbreviations and gaps... an injection of paranoia directly into the democratic process. We engage with Trump's debasements when we ask, what do they undermine? What do they hide?

In sacred Talmudic and Kabbalah traditions of interpretation, the scholar develops attentive sensitivity to multi-dimensional meaning. You learn to revere study, devoting yourself to a lifetime of education, time alone contemplating words in pursuit of the hope of finding your way to the fount of paradise, the spiritual garden of sensory renewal. Study was a healing of soul breach, the loss of common understanding that came after the Fall. Each word or sentence a kindling spark. Eventually the flame would reveal the sacramental intentions of the forms. The study of one word becomes a pathway to enlightenment. The paradise of learning was meant to lead the scholar towards the promise of restored abundance, kindly light, mending connectives in a sentence, recreating conditions for transcendent wisdom.

But a word could bewitch you with its force. And mesmerizing force can lead to arrogance, using words to blame and curse...

Here the comparisons commentators make between Trump and Hitler must be odious. Hitler was demonically eloquent. He adapted his barbaric will-to-power to polemics and pamphlets, radio and stadiums. While instinctively authoritarian and prone to abrasive racial stereotyping, Trump chose the A-literate way: the tweet voice, non-words and half-sentences spewing. Yet when we attend to one Twitter feed, we're drawn into a typo's implications and drawn into what could be a distraction from threatening, awful action.

Don't listen for long to the snake in Eden, the Angels advised Adam and Eve. Even if the babble beguiles... If you listen, you could fall into the sway of its voice. The snake is a fellow creature. The closer its presence is, and the more you accept its being, the more the malice in its voice could snare you.

Co...

vf...

e...

fe...

We could call it "A diversion for gamers." Stephen Bannon, a Trump advisor at the time of the tweet, was an entrepreneur who made millions by investing in the development of the video game "World of Warcraft." An adept of media attractions and repulsions, he recognized the hook of the virtual. On-line gaming sways senses, generating need, arousing cults and trolls.

A wrathful ideologue, Bannon promoted policies against immigrants, refugees, leftist intellectuals, Hollywood directors and ecologists. He declared war on enemies through Breitbart, his news platform until 2018. In a statement attributed to him, he said, "Politics are all logos." By *logos* he didn't mean The Word ("In the beginning was the Word..." John 1:1). He meant making slogans and headlines. He also meant mercilessly striking into the global sensibility with distracting disturbances, pouring ire into media combustion furnaces. Attribution is an effective expression of branding: if it sounds like an influential person could have said this, then whether he or she said it doesn't matter, their brand is galvanized.

The Trump tweet-typo inserted a form into both the Emoji and Emoticons: it was an iconic, punctuating moment in the media-whorl, heralding forceful moments of mainlining. It took dark turns towards manipulation and covert expression, so if there's meaning we can give to...

C o v fe fe

...then we apprehend it's an utterance reflecting
and inducing incensed emotion: a supra-text that bypasses
interpretation, racing into our baseline responses. It showed a
Twitter feeder sensing...

The rush

effects

of spurs and stings

The membrane's non-verbal space impels us with insistent
itches. We're transported into currents of effect where triggers
and prompts cause amusement and stress disorders, and where all
is posting up into the air.

Q. Have you already forgotten Covfefe?

A. Selective amnesia is part of the new cycles.

Q. Do you think it's useless, overused?

A. Where do word errors lead?
    (You could just reply, "Where-ever.")

CUE UP /
Shakeup /
The next / typos / fragments /
neologisms / blurbs

On July 2nd, 2017, we experienced another tweet pinnacle, the Day of the FNN. These letters were interpreted to mean "Fraud News Network" or "Fake News Network."
The President of the United States released an altered video—first aired in 2007—showing him pummelling a CNN reporter. A virtual figure punched a faceless body. Defacing others is a way of dehumanizing people on-line. This followed an MSNBC TV news show where a host mused on camera about Trump's sanity. His reaction was to turn news into a WWF or WWE rally. His video was a staccato hammering in data-streams that can magnify frenzy and cruelty, the hatred of calm and the addiction to combat, turning these into seductive artifice.

After /

after /

News services say, "There should be no Paywall." My translation of this pronouncement: media keep channels free even to the data-vertigo that scrambles us deeply inside the network of nerves.

And who will the media conjure and propel—through the agencies of whirl and magnetism—to speak back to Trump and his acolytes? Who'll give counter-words and counter-images?

Here the tweets and blurbs reveal again how we're entwined, meshed into closings and openings.

Thus the fierce debates about Trump in the media erupted into what critics called a data-warfare story fought over sensory bias and content.

It appeared that the print media was ganging up on the electronic media. Print media demand historical verifications, research confirmations, descriptive consistency, grammar checks and cultural memory, contexts committed to paper. Newspapers and journals thrive on a steady editorial point-of-view, the primacy of the alphabet. Learning, study, formality, and footnoting mould reading awareness. While some news services still work with literary texts and background checks, many have moved to image and bite: on-line sensation.

The electronic media flush-forward through orality, click-reverberations, "Hot Takes" (the sound-bite version of a complex thought), icons and images. It offers fast access at your fingertips, headline prompts, confrontational blogs and avatar or troll identities. This is the dynamic expressionism of everything-at-once. Borrowing and accessing information files are part of the instantaneous experience.

Both print and e-media need subscribers and advertisements to survive financially. Print media, in danger of losing ads and readers, will fan the flames by staying sensational, too. Still, newspapers close down, journals disappear. Electronica flourishes.

Print publications work on lag time, gradually edging up to the moment. Now situations shift so fast that no essayist can keep pace. Images are instant X-rays which enhance both scrutiny and blurring. Blurb-ads become both unavoidable and transient. Print allows for concentrated attention: to read deeply you need patience, calm, a room of your own, and a library close by. E-connectivity invites for speed-response: it grows with snapshots (Instagramming) that encourage mass snap protests.

Scandals about lies and false reporting in print media delight those in e-media because this proves susceptibility to corruption. Meanwhile, print editorials gloat over the conspiratorial alliances of Facebook and troll farms. Editorialists in print express demands for legal control and the protection of privacy. E-media users sensed that overrunning disembodied data is beyond control, cascading above the words of law.

And so, the data-warfare story abides.

The decisive new element (again) in this war-like condition is the role of the on-line user—bloggers, hackers. The influence and immediacy of people responding, skimming... clicking distrust and opinions about headlines and trails of data...

[img 14]

Note how the e-surges of calls for protests brought the spontaneous risings I described before... People rally into streets and arenas, quickly gathering to demonstrate against the malignant energies of racism and murderousness. Temporary marches and demonstrations often courageously struck back at the cravings for strong-man authoritarianism re-appearing in America, Russia, South Africa (long after Nelson Mandela), the Philippines, Turkey, South America (Venezuela and Brazil) and Europe (especially in Hungary and Poland). Yet people who fear the overturning of legal, constitutional order sometimes collided with those who feel the dark furor to break away from democratic states. Both were driven by the crowd cry to "take back the streets."

Democracies thrive with cries for greater participation and responsiveness. Simultaneously, democracies appear fragile, to be faltering in the crushing wake of nationalist group momentum and the contagious rage of demagogic force. Every side takes to networking platforms, twittering to make their points.

Without smartphones and Snapchat, websites and social media activism, would rallies and crowds lose much of their collectivist impetus? Protests from all places in the political spectrum have become immediate and large-scaled in their emotions.

My proposal: the ideal for the sensorium is gestalt of the alphabet and e-media, reading and scanning in a fearful symmetry. This would apprehend the data-warfare between print and screen in terms of complementarity, *The Media Marriage of Heaven and Hell,* in William Blake's terms. Meaning: print-paper experience needs high-voltage events for inspiration and requires measured time to reflect on their significance; digital media need hyper-texting speed, the jump from atom to atom, site to site, its gaps calling for the contemplations of print sensibility.

Is one law for print and screen a tyranny?

The data-warfare metaphor preserves the either-or (us versus them) premise. How do we (how do I) get past this codified structuring, into infinite malleability, into compassion for our many sides, the complex ways we perceive, receive...

I submit: print and screen must depend on each other, the complement a marriage of Kabbalah and Alchemy, print and electronic media metamorphosing into renewing configurations of effects. Thus solitude and collectivity may mingle.

These complementary effects reflect the openings and closings in our immersive time of emerging mythologies. "We're following the stories..." on-line and TV commentators announce.

Like aspiring soothsayers staring into teacup dregs and palms, we look into images and propagating tweets, the screens sometimes taken for crystal balls. The screens are full of pixels and intimations, and we intuit that the membrane's manifestations make the fables of Homer, Hesiod, Virgil and Ovid look like crumbling plaster busts, and any rigid rationale like a parched page, in an antique museum located in a forgotten desert village about to be buried under sand and ashes...

The present a vast attraction

a vast repulsion

we go back and forth in the dynamo

Let us look at more expressions of the print-electronic Marriage of Heaven and Hell.

Former President Barack Obama showed that he could speak on the mythic planes of instantaneous media coverage. Adroit with symbolism, moderate if cautious in his policies, he addressed the waves of emotion and of intellect during his two election campaigns. Observe Obama's use of the pause in his public speeches. This was a way of tempering events, slowing down pulsations.

He was criticized for being "professorial" (too detailed) and detached ("No-Drama Obama," newspaper headlines labelled him). All leaders falter. What matters is the momentum in consciousness and subconscious stirrings that a leader represents and inspires, promotes and routes, defuses and redirects, incites, inflames. It's Obama's poise that we're likely to remember.

Michelle Obama showed she understood media agency: she could speak to emotion and intellect simultaneously. Her supporters encouraged her to run in an American federal election. She'd likely defeat Trump or the acolytes that would appear to continue his form of resentful, merciless spectacle. However, her candidacy would bring vital controversies. These would reveal what is—for us in the grip of the www/http state of emergency and alert—a nostalgia for dynastic lineage (royalty) and an attachment to the screen glow of charisma.

Do dynastic links and image charm embody a tendency towards anti-democratic and repressive undercurrents in the charge? The appeal of dynasty could become a showcase for continuity through heraldic wealthy families and billionaire leadership: someone steps up for you, supposedly representing your interests, one who appears to have a background in apprehending the dark-light energies of the openings and closings...

During the 2016 American federal election campaign, Trump masked that he was an oligarch speaking for other oligarchs, the influences we call "Dark Money." He appeared "out of his mind": incoherence was a lead strategy. Translation: he was authentically tactless, the presumed outsider relishing public and virtual responses to escalating predatory claims.

Essayists and critics reacted to his transparency by calling it a void. They couldn't see how he charged up audiences who believed that his going to the abyss edge was the sign that transformation must come at any cost. Eloquence and learning were suspect because they appeared to be activities of the old literary, pre-live-tweet paradigm. Bring down the system of self-entitled insiders, he promised during his campaign. "Drain the swamp!" the shout rose.

Hillary Clinton seemed to embody common sense, the insider's view. She proved to be too careful for the tingling of incessant stimulation. Bewildered by the Trump tweet-blitz and stand-up, Clinton reverted to her habitual secrecy, becoming opaque, because she was uncomfortable in the spotlight of Super PAC and social media INFO-wars, evasive about her intrigues and shady financial affiliations (she was trailing clouds of suspicion), therefore a candidate who could, once elected, be potentially "under constant investigation." "Lock her up," the chants went.

Any expression of a middle way will be unpopular when the pull of extremism—magnetic polar opposites—takes hold. Anyone who maintains a private mask in the Circus Maximus appears to be hiding something from the anarchic-satiric sites of disclosure available through the web. A person in the media spotlight risks being shut off, and called "boring," if she or he doesn't scintillate.

Let's bring our readings and scans to Canada.

Justin Trudeau became the positive mirror image of the malign negating Trump. Justin channelled the electronic media effectively and intuitively, too. Another media icon, he represented our hyper-evolutionary conditions, appearing on our screens of fate (inevitability) and destiny (possibility).

We saw how intertwined he was with the web sensations of social media when he strayed from prepared speeches. He sounded hesitant veering between the scripted and the unscripted. Note his "ums" and "uhs," his jittery intake of breath when he spoke in English. This reflected what could have been a nervous reaching for a sound bite. Tense moments rob us of breath. When Justin spoke in French, he was smoother (calmed, calming).

He entered the media-whorl to encourage us with sunny ways: lightness. When he succeeded, he offered images of steady, amiable concern. When he faltered, the lightness became shallow. Though apologetic, and sensitive, he was another adept intuiting that governing by communications is about mood and branding appearances.

Beyond ideological, he tried to steer a wary way through the middle of our global epic of polarized positions of the right and left. Make no mistake: the middle way doesn't refer to preserving the status quo at any cost. It summons progressive awareness through the recognition of pluralism. At its best, the middle way is the way of wisdom, respecting complexity, resisting inertia and predatory impulses, and collectivist and nationalist extremism.

It's an open story whether any political party through symbolism and access to populist grievances could counter the presence of the amiable leader and the apologetic tone. Over time we'll see if photo-op charisma will be enough to counter Trump's unhinged corporatism and bragging contempt for literary eloquence. People muttering about Justin's stamina and courage in the darting arc of sensory mood swings, from emotional irritability and the craving for authoritarianism to empowering visions of citizen participation... Amiability can appear like a lack of backbone. Still, intuitive understanding and an even temper shouldn't be underestimated. His story and his quest will unfold in exemplary ways...

Justin's charisma had to differ from that of his father, former Prime Minister Pierre Elliott Trudeau. Certainly, their last name ensured the dynastic link. But Pierre Trudeau was a literary person, a shrewd and private sensibility with considerable gravitas who could paradoxically, flippantly play with what was new media then (radio, black-and-white TV).

Pierre Trudeau opposed militant nationalism and extremist
populism in their many guises. He was a political essayist shaped
by the proposals of liberal democratic thinkers John Stuart Mill and
Isaiah Berlin, and by the Personalist thought of Catholic theologian
Emmanuel Mounier and the evolutionary hope of Teilhard de Chardin.
My paraphrase of his ideas: each person has value; there's necessity
in the cultivations of inwardness; you must bear witness to your time;
liberty is essential, but unfettered liberty can turn destructive; the
championing of complexity and pluralism—recognizing that many
views coexist—is a moral imperative; enlightenment requires a
vigilant engagement with the body politic. Separatism is the sterile
denial of the bond of the human family.

Would he be electable in our shimmering, supra-attentive
atmosphere? In our time's pressures and forms, people who are
bruised and lacerated, terrified and lonely, call for apologies...
People also struggling with purpose, with self-interest... Would he
understand how Canada is at a crossroads where the alliances born of
the separatist debates of the 1960s through to the 90s are morphing
(hurtling) into debates (on-line, in town halls) about religious-
political symbolism and deep worry, multi-lingual populations and
collective rights?

Advice to readers: another pause for thought...

People are told not to publish or post long broodings or reflections in the public domains of book and screen, especially not on the web, because few have the time or the concentration to read them. Attention spans are drawn to the brief interval, the turn (and return) to screen magnetism and its ionic agitations.

ADD has become a natural state of reception

And where do we jump next?

In what form are you scanning this?

I'm writing and reading in freefall

(And if we could sit still; and if we could unplug and breathe... Meditating, breathing... We'd nourish our dreaming, our reveries: maybe we'd absorb the magnetism—the pull into the polarizing, the extremes.)

Let us go then you and I

Texting in the scattering

Fusions of hyper-speed

(And do you remember books? The tangible pages, the slightly musty smell, how they were bound, the effect of type on your eye, the alphabet's presence, the white space surrounding the letters. Opening a book, you opened yourself.

...I remember being alone and over time holding in my hands Of Time and the River, The Waves, The Sound and the Fury, Wuthering Heights, Don Quixote, Leaves of Grass, *and* Four Quartets. *Through the years I followed the passages into the stubborn books that made such demands. These books couldn't be exhausted. Difficulties, densities: the transport of their open spaces delved into me, drawing me inwards and forwards into their words and sentences. And always there was the sense of the story behind them, the Spirit that drove their depths, what won't falter and fade, what passes on, between the lines, inside the words.)*

Streaming skimming

Within you and without you

Anywhere nowhere

Reflecting more on Gaia

and the communications' envelope, on how quickly our minds and sensibilities have transformed in the membrane's evolutionary jumpstart... Associations: one of the effects of pollution is smog, with its corrosive impact on health and perception. You can choke on poisoned air. What's called brain-fog may close down sensory and mental experience, resulting in blurriness, dizziness, inability to concentrate, absent-mindedness, blank-outs in attention, coughing fits, migraines, nervousness, numbing, loss of inspiration... Breathing is symbolically linked to inspiration, receiving the air of influence. And inspiration is an opening: welcoming images and ideas so that you begin again. "Kardices" is the word for the sacred place of the heart in theology and poetics. It's also the origin of the medical term "cardiac." Observe how information excess can bring a kind of pollution, a smudging of attention and awareness. Notice how people are instructed to overcome chatter and clogging by "listening to the heart."

Journalists and editorialists scathingly speak of the crisis of "Dumbing Down" in the electronic news domains. Truly what's at play is a combination of the sensational widening of apprehension and a form of Traumatic Stress Syndrome—"Numbing Down," we should call it. The latter brings the limiting of our intake valves of sensitivity and consciousness.

Climate change deniers confine their opinions to what they already know, repudiating evidence and discovery. Yet can we say that shutting down is the fall-back position of most people? How often does opinion replace exploration? It's then we let habit and already established frames take over from engagements off the prescribed routes. (These frames are often called News Silos.) Data gluts can freeze responses into formulae. "Don't confuse me with the facts. My mind is made up." The cliché is telling. It's hard to get lost or to perceive directly when Google Maps, or a prescription, is nearby...

...though the wilderness or frontier, whether Natural or part of electronic Supra-Nature, will take you places you can't recognize or describe yet...

...the wilderness is often called our heartland...

...and when we go into the frontier of nerve-ends and receptions, the wild turbulence we create and apprehend—we dive...

[img16]

into the boundless oscillations of the communal flux
and light-dark energies...

the unspoken, wavering places, energies that seem
beyond the reach of familiar markers...

Paranoia

is heightened perception, mania becoming a source
for insights. When communications swift-current
around the planet, paranoia can be an instrument
for feeling what is looming and apprising what is
unfamiliar. It taps into the invisible currents.

Derangement has its uses. It's a way
of staving off numbing. But great enthusiasm
can reel into wild anxiety when prompted by
the sense that unseen powers drive you. "You hide,
they seek," says "Proverbs for Paranoids, 4" in Thomas
Pynchon's Gravity's Rainbow.

Communications can seem covert. Something's on the
verge... Nearing. What's here? Paranoia is the reverse side of
acute sensitivity. If all things meld in speeding mutuality, then
it's just a quick about-face to see everything impending. The rule
of suspicion thus appears...

Conspiracy theories swarm in the gaps between the print
medium and the electronica of sensation and heated headlines.
Still, descriptions that fully match facts are impossible outside
of science and mathematics. Not even Quantum Mechanics, with
its beautifully strange evocations of subatomic realities, has a
language that maps what we can't see. Imagination and opinion
must play a part. We remake more than we itemize or verify. Now
we're remaking in conditions of iCloud and access overdrive.

"Shift Happens," wry graffiti announces. What happens when a leader insists that his take on reality is the only one? This is a way that a leader or a movement turns authoritarian. Possibilities are contained in a monolithic view. *"I alone..."* Trump announced during his election campaign. *"In the end you will thank me..."* Trump said during the first months of his presidency after another magnetizing and demagnetizing act (the meaning of polarization). Recall the prophetic caption accompanying the joke-image of a car teetering on a cliff-edge: "Who are you going to believe... your GPS or your own eyes?"

Data bubbles insulate users, habituating them to closed circuits. This provokes hyper-states of awareness that ramp up assent and anxiety.

Cartoon-like conspiracy theories become frenzied when lonely people fear the complexities lurking in static, oscillations, dash and blur, the prompts and press of replicating data. The visible disorder must be overshadowed by a singular order not apparent to everyone. Networks sending-receiving information can seemingly traffic in a simple weird, dangerous intention. Invisible currents invite the hyperbole of conspiracy theorizing, the mind operating "outside of itself." This is pattern-recognition flipping into paranoia.

People adept at reading patterns often claim they have special second-sight (insight, foresight)—an occult seeing into the gaps of static where things seem hidden. Invisibility, cloaking, become obsessions for people hyper-attentive to collective media activity: What's out there? Who's filling up my mailbox with requests for replies?

Sleeplessness and panic, bombast and insensitivity incite internet alternative worlds in which threats and accusations run rampant. Philip K. Dick's dystopian visions of overlapping psychotic realities and controlling voices invading consciousness now seem routine. *Electric Dreams* is the pointed title the Space TV producers gave to their 2017 adaptations of Dick's prophetic stories. In Dick's writings something huge skulks behind everything that happens.

Democracies become vulnerable in such skittish conditions. People feel harassed, battered, but also tuned out, blasé. Who'll stop the reign of speed? Some say, "Who cares?" The faster things go, the more events flick into ephemeral caricatures. Speed feeds numbing out and fatigue, the sense that things are over-heated and over-saturated.

This is when cult leaders make their pitch, and their money: they call to starved people, supply meaning to lonely seekers, give permission to suspicions, put on shows. Those who make voracious Twitter claims see themselves becoming searing leaders of mass movements, welcoming the formation of followers and rallies. *"I will solve your problems for you…"* Denunciation takes the place of argument. *"Our enemies are everywhere and want to stop our movement…"* These are sound bites and biddings that herald the urge towards authoritarianism, the energy attracting people who feel crushed, drained, abandoned and aggrieved.

Let us look into data breaching. This occurs with instant exposés and informing what we see in alternative sourcing.

Do hackers, satellite-cable radio hosts (shock jocks), trolls and blog-satirists and their dark posts possess elements in common? They channel and reroute the impact of the charging flux. In their most extreme expressions they want to infiltrate it with their force and burn up the worldwide membrane. Many are the shock troops of the currents and its signals. More than ever are appearing. It's another sign of the membrane's influence, its pulsating embrace…

There are, of course, subtle differences in how hackers, smear trolls, shock jocks and dark-post satirists experience the charge. Some participate through speaking, talking (in the air); some sit in front of screens for hours, days, nights (tapping, touching keyboards); some are on their own; some work for corporations or governments.

Importantly, shock jocks and trolls come in a variety of shades. Sometimes they're nihilists, stomping on values. They may be ideological zealots eager to distort outcomes of democratic elections. Blog-satirists can be comedians, witty editorialists commenting memorably on the stupidities of the day. Some are canny moralists, who hope that the vulnerability and availability of the worldwide sensorium will awaken us to enlightenment. Satirist-bloggers can be visionaries of social political mores who have the imperative of wanting you to see what's right there in front of you.

But when we examine the phenomena of the disruptors, we find corresponding fields in the digital streams: acceptance of the membrane's presence; migrations into its nets; recognition of the fluidity and speed-up of its transformations; the plunge into its attractions and repulsions; the plug-ins becoming arousing intoxicants; nomadic out-of-body experiences (dematerialization when roving the airwaves); the realization of how close we are in webs where voices and images mutate; the sensation of being unbound, that we're elevated by limitless realities through information saturations and cloaked identities; cultivations of cult droves around the world who share the furies. Many want to directly enter minds and sensibilities to permeate our cells, altering them. There's the feeling that in their hands, in their voices, they have uncanny force, a supernatural capacity to intervene.

It's in the venomous dosing of this unleashed iconoclasm that we find the sharing of attitudes and approaches. We see injections of cynicism, the altering of reports and files, the recasting of history and records to suit a purpose, and the poisonous verbal outpouring they call "truth-telling." The cynicism comes from the sense that some believe they have absolute ownership of unfiltered facts. Abuse-Hate Messaging is another sign of dark judgments and click-opinions coursing into our lives.

Data breaching is akin to satiric iconoclasm and conspiratorial paranoia. It brings extreme levels of attention to data or systems that are being withheld or protected, encrypted or monopolized by someone, or something, behind the masks of power. Sometimes hackers and trolls believe their disruptions and distractions are meant to be instructive. Their loyalty is often to shadowy fellow on-line users who share the sense of being overpowered, and not to those participating in what they perceive to be the insidious machinations of politics. Sometimes their breaches are criminal, attacks on government itself.

Satiric jabs can be a freeing of energy: a necessary purgation. Satirists fight repressions in us and the suppression of news. The privilege of satire is found in relieving laughter. The danger: satiric lines of attack can become a way of coarsening response, part of the blunting and the shuttering of perspectives so that only a very few get the spoofs. Satirists often assault the tyrannical and get their rush from becoming themselves tyrannically powerful, listing people's faults, delivering verdicts, penalizing, condemning, punishing, ostracizing.

"Naming & Shaming" and "Naming & Blaming" refer to the net turning into a tribunal and confessional. Informing, humiliating, admitting, calling out, refusing... This is sometimes called doxing...

Breached data could burn you up at the stake, your reputation reduced to cinders. Note the words "informs" and "informers." Their ambiguities and associations show how we can be insiders (inside the forms), massaged (reformed or managed by data-flow), anonymous betrayers (revealing sources or government codes) and whistle-blowers (performing services to the body communicant).

[img17]

The communal experience of magnetism and spin may sharpen the allure of hacking, smear-trolling, shock jockeying, dark-post blogging. Many move in a coded insurgency against the global membrane becoming the homeland of a common humanity, the Cosmopolis of the Spirit. Our evolutionary jump into empathic networks can be perceived to be coercive and levelling. It also gives an opportunity to splice and cut: snap at the strands of the electrical connections by using the connectors...

Against the communing, the transforming transmissions that come immediately into us, trolls and shock jocks lure you with danger, ravening zeal, the force of certainty and the seductions of hatred and aggression towards perceived perpetrators and plots, fluid alliances. We note how hackers often become spearheads of ultra-nationalist-separatist movements.

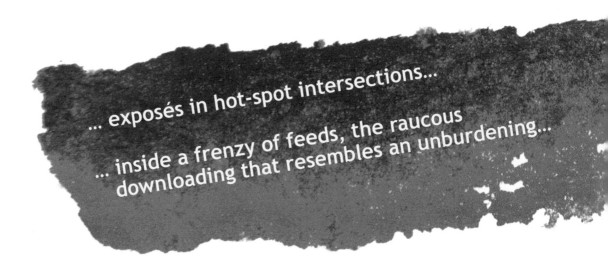

... exposés in hot-spot intersections...

... inside a frenzy of feeds, the raucous downloading that resembles an unburdening...

Observe again how the sensory effect of abrasive disclosures by the disruptors can bring a petrifying to the soul: hyper-insensitivity rather than greater sensitivity. The polarizations whetted by a remorseless rage may trigger brutal purges that end up boosting the vexed or aggravated screen-centres and the addiction to extremism. And when iconoclasm veers into preying, and when some want to send lightning bolts into wired-up already nervous communicating channels, any decency, or so-called netiquette, must collapse...

NOISY ATTACKS

AREN'T HARD TO FIND...

BUT COULD YOU CATCH THE SILENT

ATTACKER LURKING BENEATH THE SURFACE...

USING ARTIFICIAL INTELLIGENCE   DARKTRACE FINDS

THE QUIET CYBERTHREATS

INSIDE YOUR

ORGANIZATION

DARKTRACE DETECTS IT   AND FIGHTS BACK

IN REAL TIME

We thus surmise that web disrupters increase vilifying and demeaning energies. Through the venom, threats and conspiracy theories become palpable, felt in our portals, on our sites.

It's possible there's an authentic cathartic aspect to the discharges. Still, wisdom traditions (I'm thinking of the Kabbalah) counsel us to be circumspect about word-spells, what we unbridle when we speak and write. We see users turning from thrilling private simulations (internet fantasies) to stimulating instants that foment terrifying animosities. The malevolent voices incite barbarism, cursing us with more unease. People call this virulent atmosphere the fear-scape.

Note how trolls and hackers often stay unaccountable, becoming untraceable (disappearing into invisible currents). Some cite a free speech defence—a vestige of alphabetic consciousness, the time when letters predominated. But their injections no longer have a source in human complexities and sympathies, blunting kindness by pitilessly merging with the effects of orbiting satellites, winging up into the cold stratosphere where disembodied transmissions and signals can cross and war.

Look to clichés and viral repetitions of statements for insights about states of response and reation.

Everyone feels the static cling—the impress of particles—and so we become touchy. Tempers flare, sore memories spill, nerve-ends jump, emotions frazzle, positions become inflexible: vulgarity and spite become habitual: debates turn unforgiving and accusatory. People in left-right political camps become faster at taking or giving offence. Lawsuits are filed over the unlicensed theft of personal images. People continually post apologies for the harm they've done to others. Speakers must ask for permission to talk about certain subjects. Those who callously insult others in the workplace are asked to participate in Sensitivity Training. Meanwhile, newspapers blaze headlines about threats to free speech.

The membrane's pulsations extend irritations and offended sensibilities and at the same time the desire for tranquility and peace. Observe the proliferation of yoga studios in cities and towns, places where people stretch out and tone their bodies to relax. "Show your heart," yogis say, "Show it to the sky and remember to breathe... Open your mind and let your day fall away from you." This soothes the pressures we feel on our skin. Notice too how people like to withdraw into meditative time of listening to music with noise-cancelling headphones. A planet of excited messaging concentrates billions of eyes and ears, scanning, eaves-dropping, tuning in and sometimes seeking healing atonements through talking cures, lessons, advice, webinars and conversations with strangers who are quickly befriended. "Atoning" and "attuning" are closely related etymologically.

And 24-7 we audit

the omnidirectional soundscapes

of the Noosphere

Alarm bells go off, sirens whoop, doorbells sound, cellphones jingle, intercoms trill, drive-by songs play... Clock-towers chime, halogen lights fizz and buzz... Fridges and microwaves step up subliminal static...

Cars sluice by in a highway distance... Roadways, traffic jamming seemingly getting nearer all the time... Helicopters and jets circle and streak with their thudding and rumbling... Police drones glide humming overhead...

AI voices in Bluetooth-Echo devices promptly reply to your requests ("Hi, I'm Alexa... What would you like to hear?"), and program Smart-Homes... Impatience may have a sensory source: too much sound could make you fidgety.

Excessive noise can also contribute to sensations of dizziness and claustrophobia: everything seems to be closing in, seizing up. Low frequencies (turbines, pile drivers) alter bio-rhythms and ocean currents, causing alterations in the faring habits and echo-locational sensitivity of animals and fish. Neurologists say people who experience hearing loss through environmental stresses are prone to headaches and tinnitus.

"Don't become de-sensitized...," a CNN editorialist warned...

[img 18]

Yet many in Generations X, Y, and Z, those who are Millennials, Xennials, Net-gens, seem to have adapted to the soundwaves and electroscapes, becoming thriving pilgrims in the info-surf. Here's a sampling that shows the adaptation of our bodies to sonic permeations: the popular phenomenon of tattooing reveals the desire to imprint the charge's pulsations on your skin. Tattoos impress the body with design mediations linking you to others who feel the same way: you show empathic solidarity. Your flesh is punctured and illustrated; tattoos acknowledge that you're receiving, your skin matters. People learning to telegraph the magic of signals on their bodies, absorbing the pricks and points of info-influxes, listening in, staying sensitive...

Consider this: contrast the tattoo absorptions onto skin with the sound of blows. What troubles the atmosphere from tweets and blogs... this is the bruising effect, the concussive harm done to the senses by the slaps and punches of verbal reaming and viciousness...

Developing story—still more to come—

...The CNN editorial warning was apt, after the global village and theatre and the Circus Maximus were subsumed into the vibrant membrane.

Now listen to the howl

To the Silence Breaking

#MeToo   Her   Personal & Communal   Cry

Sofia Shekinah breaking chains holding her down

The ghosts of electricity howling

In the bones of her face

Rising with Gaia's suffering

There's   a charge   A charge.

For the hearing   of her   heart

Ms.   Under Standing Me Dia

The banner announced over the door

At the McLuhan Centre

Toronto   December 2017

The voice that carries wounds

When all is circulating pouring

Demanding hearings   participation mystique

Her outcry   Her rebellion

Against choked confines   Gagging

Imprisoned livid soul

Calling out the sense of   Violation

Invasion   Interference   Division

Pushing back at the Reactive-Insult Currency

#MeToo   Silent No More

This is live witnessing   life witnessing   since 2017

Female energy impassioned

Electrification streaming through

Sensitivity to touch

Impelling us to consider

What have we done   To silence   One   Others

Listen   A voice breaking

What does her openness dare us   to

Know   Time's Up

Is there a surge   seductive   invasive in images

Images we don't fully fathom

We're bare

Voyagers   and questors

In the wires jangling   rivers murmuring

Screens speaking   trees leaning into the wind

Smartphones ringing   the sun moon vibrating light

Texting addressing   stars in their frequencies

Pressing Send   Pressing Save   Save ourselves

The membrane echoes the cosmos full of voices

Images spreading   disseminating

Where how do you stand in the intimacy

Stream   flow   pulse   flux

Hyper-data pressing us

While she's telling and confessing to the whorl

What it means to be bare

"It's a warlock hunt, not a witch-hunt" a post says

There are dangers of accusation   Revenge

But the voice calling to be heard over data-mass

The airing requires hearings   Time's Up

Breaking taboos leads to unsealing

Removal of muffling   leading to   wildfire

Moments   awakening us

To our obsessive image-making

Endlessly seductive in its exhibitionist availability

Erotica furor

Combustible energy-fields

This is just the beginning

No secure lines in the membrane

All stored in clouds   No delete button

Discharging must also bring   deep   scars to light

(bestowing   flickering)

And gravity

(crucial awareness of   suffering)

Seeking illuminations

In the charges

That usher testimonials

And   repentance

Her voice in the light-pulse

Exposing our capacity for projection on others

And demanding that we soul-search

The effects

[img19]

What   What did we do to perpetuate the pain

This is   Just   the beginning

What have you done   What have I

In our sense-surround, the miracle of sympathetic vibrations and impressionability must stay alive by listening to differing voices, and by cultivating spaces of inwardness and reflection.

It's essential for us to find time for contemplating and intuiting, for practising restful periods, dialling down the noise-smears, piecing together the news from many sources, for a dissidence to counter the poison and the unfettered cravings of pumped-up leaders and trolls, for developing the skill to recognize hyper-nervous patterns with compassion and good will, meeting people who are suffering, stopping our rush around to be at the side of others. It's a lot to ask of ourselves. Speeding is easy, resting is hard. Where will we know stillness? When will we find moments to reflect?

Stories circulate, on the web, in cable documentaries, about the desire to become quieter. Witness the proliferation of Wave-Free Zones in airports, areas where handheld communication devices are forbidden. This is an ecology policy for the senses that recognizes that our receptive capacities, our feelings, are being permeated and overwhelmed.

And there are stories about our desire to become introspective, finding stillness. Witness the appearance of tiny rental houses: "Compact Cabins" that offer the sensory refreshment of unplugging. These are sparse meditative spaces in getaway caravans located in rustic areas. Here you must pay for the privilege of solitude. Still, the tiny houses provide light and heat.

In safe homes, realtors sell cloistered spaces set aside from stressors—texting, screens, debt-loads, stimulants, excess—for depleted people to hold books in their hands or to talk softly to one another. These sanctuary places recall Emily Dickinson's small room in her family's home, the poet's window on the certain slant of light— "The Soul selects her own Society—Then—shuts the Door—" But by her window Dickinson was keen, shuddering. Isolation was dissent, liberation for her.

You huddle in the hush of a retreat, looking for pared-down periods; and so for a time you can be bypassed. The rooms seem to make it easier to shape and clarify messaging currents, the cellular sway of interlinking networks. These inward movements into safe zones seek to restore and preserve receptivity to affect, the quiver of response stunned by waves, stunted by accumulating data-clouds.

But can we escape the flux? Is it possible to evade the currents and clouds, even if openings bring wounds and rages? Let us compare milieus. We'll know truth by comparing environments and stories. Peaceful zones may help to slow down the heart-pulse rate in our jittery fervour and soul exposures.

Let me write now on a different wave-length, recalling the experience that was once called Literature.

Note how many authors opted out of the wired wireless, avant-garde spectacle: Alice Munro, Don DeLillo, Elena Ferrante, Thomas Pynchon, Cormac McCarthy, Anne Carson, Marie-Claire Blais, Marilynne Robinson, Harold Bloom, sometimes trying to elude, or deflect, the effects of absorbing media. Ironically, this becomes a media tale, too. It became a legend that neither Ferrante nor Pynchon wished to be photographed. Munro, McCarthy, DeLillo, and Carson gave rare, prized interviews that revealed almost nothing about themselves or their craft. Susan Howe composed her oracular *Debths* to preserve gnomic difficulties. A reader must become a diviner of her word-intensities, and the spirals and dots that trace like atoms across her pages... They conserved needful solitude, their essential depths, by exiling themselves from what may appear like mobbing noise and cliché, turning away from web-clogging that can push reductive misinformation.

Authors turn to the margins, going into a quiet underground, the resistance of books, where they can work slowly, safe-guarding their sense and sensibility, cultivating their vocations, restoring the rendezvous with seclusion and truth's complexities... Privacy has come to mean nurturing shelter, slowing down time, redirecting the velocity and the inductions into cyber-heat, vacating radiation networks.

Reading has become for some another alternative imaginative space, a retiring from hyper-intensities: a way to allay addled nerves.

And yet when we read a book we call for hushed periods so we may find sustained attentiveness to the beautiful ambiguities of words, and the shiver and gleam of allusive sentences, so we can concentrate and listen to the elusive flame of the spirit on the printed page, suddenly visible in the incandescent moments of our refining appreciation and awakened time.

(Does this mean Literature has become a nowhere-land whose only watchwords are now Style and Story?)

With the turning inwards, literary space becomes smaller: observe the obsession in contemporary fiction, drama, poetry and essays with rooms, towns, interior monologues, family breakdowns, individual hurts and crack-ups, trekking alone through a wilderness...

Academia has long been a subsidized retreat for sustained, secluded reflections on writing and reading. We find authors withdrawing into academia (I'm one of them), often writing melancholic marginalia—fragments, annotations on established literary works... Splinters in page-fringes... Musings in shadow-pages...

Marginalia is a collaborative art form. Recall Blake's spikey annotations to Wordsworth's thought, Coleridge's pencil scrawls in the white spaces of his beloved books, Dickinson's daring hand-scrawls on envelopes of letters that may not have been mailed, H.D.'s ciphers marking up the margins of the books she studied on the occult. Insertions and underscoring become nuanced epics of personal engagement: to meet and resurrect your spiritual mentors' words is a quest for inspiring company. If people are reading books less and less, then those who write them will seek companionship in the presences that reveal, or conceal, themselves between the lines of type.

We find literary theorists writing their way out of desperate loneliness—the sense of being marginalized into ascetic quarantine—by constructing discourses cast in a framing jargon that must be annotated and footnoted by fellow theorists.

Cultural scenes, mostly in large cities, become inevitably cozy. This parallels the contraction of literary space into a small sphere of intensified scrutiny. Who is reading? ... Who is your audience? The institutions of publishing talk about target or niche marketing. Coterie-driven, literati introversion is the implicit recognition that few people read books outside of the circles of reputation. These withdrawals are understandable. After all, those who prefer solitude and complexity, to be in book time, need a person to talk to once in a while.

Still, the turn towards inwardness registers a fear of the sensory shifts in the cell-mass. Anxiety and resistance stir when fertile emissions and immense vibrations move consciousness into uncommon moments. New appearances swirl. Moods rise, fall. Writing and reading call you into retreats... The flux in the channels pairs spectacle and cloisters...

Paradoxically, quixotically, these preserving privacies and hermetic retreats hide in the open: they're easy to see.

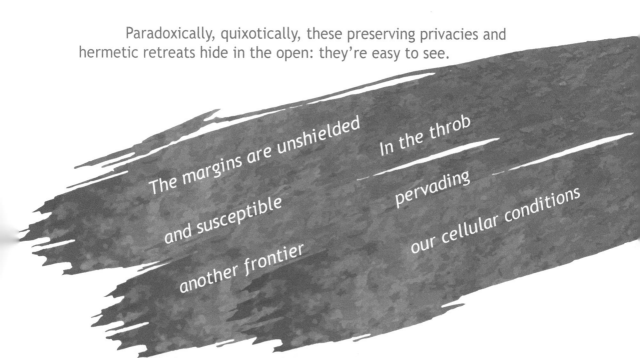

The margins are unshielded
and susceptible
another frontier

In the throb
pervading
our cellular conditions

CHINA LAKE

Fe   HART
SANDI STUTZ /   ARNER / RED CAHO
Director, Scr   ARQUARDT.
Editor CH   R WEIHL.
M
Running Time   Production Pocasso Studios. San Francisco, CA
Titles and Graphics EMIGRE GRAPHICS

I'M TIRED OF MEN I WANT GOD

This is the story of our moment...

The doors of perception have been ripped off their hinges in data-web saturations. Meaning: we're not standing on one side of a door or another. All is hum, hack, flicker, tweet, leak, feed, livestream, buzz and more buzz. There's permeating excitement, engulfment of the senses—the dynamo generating elation and a shrinking, or shuddering, from the impact.

On the satellite station E Street Radio, Bruce Springsteen described our immersion in the universal systole and diastole: "On the radio airwaves, our souls converge around one sound and one idea..." (I heard this one day, fleetingly, while driving my car, in December 2017.) These are the dynamics of becoming headlong, gathering in the momentum, wedded to what is happening not just to you or me, to us or them, but wholly to we.

Receptivity and grace are linked to the impulsions that could lead to shut-down and pain: we may say, "It's not clear enough" (bring on more vision, transparency); we may say, "It's all too much" (tilt).

Selfies are birth certificates and passport photos in the borderless-ness, the exoduses and pilgrimages in the membrane. They confirm we exist—in digital archives, high in the clouds— and that we're witnesses, here, there, somewhere, anywhere, everywhere.

IMs... what techies call Instant Messaging. A translation of the acronym: I'm singular, I'm multitudes. Each person a mediator in the flow of the one and the many: each of us a member of the mobility, the volatility, the beat, the chorus.

Epigraph 2

"*Myself compu—*
ted were they pearls
What legacy
could be"

Emily Dickinson, *Envelope Poems*

Now, if you're still with me, here are baby-boomer reflections, musings on cultural figures of my time who transformed the charge into poetry and furnished the soul with beauty.

Come along...

I'll share my enthusiasms...

...and express my gratitude to those, our visionary companions, who opened themselves to the currents...

Bob Dylan, Leonard Cohen, Patti Smith, David Bowie and Joni Mitchell were pioneers of the raw flux, the fire's momentum, filtering and distilling its galvanizing feeds. Cusp-artists, experts in shamanistic transformations, they created works in the interfaces of book culture and the mass reach of radio, hi-fi, TV and amplified concerts, moving between the domains of songs, theatre, visual art, videos, prose and poetry. Inspired by the moment when shape-shifting became available through the electronic instant...

...theirs is a story of awakened sensitivities stirring to the sounds, codes, images, and letters, the beat of fast-time metamorphoses. They had prescient insight into how the global village was about to become the global theatre then the burning circuits of the Genesis overdrive.

Bob Dylan moved into the opening time by recognizing the power of radio and phonographs: many voices travelling through the atmosphere. He tapped into the inspiration of multitudes, the migrations of sounds, and became simultaneously present and evasive, recording LP after LP yet rooting himself in privacy. "I'm Not There" is the name of the 2007 film about him, where six actors play different aspects of his complicated personae.

He became an originator by melding folk-rock with defiance of predictability and privilege, and by joining theology (the long fall, the triumphant rise) with masterly lyrical rhyming. A liberating solo artist, he spoke for collective journeys. "How does it feel / to be on your own?" his most famous song called to radioactive listeners. The subconscious choral reply to the refrain of "Like a Rolling Stone" is "We're with you / searching together..."

His interviews became over the years art-forms—put-ons of insolent eloquence, of stubborn ironies. They're also rich in storytelling and gracious tributes to fellow musicians.

Dylan said, "Everything I sing is a love song." He spoke that time without irony. Inside his protest songs there were the seeds of his later songs: the desire to reach through to loving homages, the release of his stranger's sensibility, his isolate state of mind, into poetic union. This impressionable mass media troubadour sang in his way for the one and many.

Chronicles Volume 1 is an indispensable work that tells us how attuned Dylan is to technological environments and their effects, especially those coming from radio and LPs. He recalls how radio lifted his spirit into the ether's vibrations. Everything in the airwaves is concurrent with the republic of the imagination. He describes how a recording studio's ambience in New Orleans altered the moods and pacing of his songs. He makes it clear that he wanted both to enthrall listeners and to avoid the determining press of crowds.

And his autobiography reveals how truly concealed he remains: he gives little away about his soul's state.

Will there be a *Volume 2?* Maybe... Maybe not... Elusiveness, complexity, paradox and ambiguity are Dylan's ways of staying alive artistically.

The Nobel Prize conferred on Dylan in 2016 was peculiarly controversial, annoying many observers. I say "peculiar," because the award confirmed the obvious. Dylan's genius enhanced the acoustic-poetic consciousness of the cosmic amphitheatre where he, and the Beatles, led the way in the electrification of the bardic arts.

"In the electronic age we are living entirely by music," McLuhan said in his off-hand way that concealed and revealed volumes. Dylan's prize was a signal from the literary establishment that McLuhan's maxim was true. (Even if the award came too late: it should have been awarded decades earlier.)

Dylan retrieved the tribal seer: the Homeric epic and Sapphic lyric rooted in the oral. He became a multimedia artist long before the definition existed. Adept at conversion, he's been a painter, performer, actor, archivist, radio host, author, activist, quiet recluse, singer of classic American songs; he changed his name from Zimmerman to Dylan in a tribute to Dylan Thomas; he was a born-again Christian who flipped back to Judaism and back to Christianity and back to Judaism. All is possible in the immediacy and reverberations of our musical-mutable states. He knew from the beginning of his singing-composing life that the literary specialist (the book-bound I, discrete, isolated) had been obsolesced (another word for marginalized).

Dylan replied to the news of the prize with enigmatic silence. Then he emailed a terse telegram of thanks. He avoided going to the ceremony. He sent Patti Smith to sing his warning song, "A Hard Rain's A-Gonna Fall." To her embarrassment, she flubbed the lyrics and had to restart before staid Nobel guests and Swedish royals. Then he responded with more silence.

He gave his required Nobel speech months later in the United States. Media reporters and academics pounced when they saw how the speech was in part plagiarized from on-line sources. ...Another elusive act? Was it his impish acknowledgment that sources can be—and have always been—collective or anonymous?

He said in his notes to his debut LP, *Bob Dylan*, in 1962: "Some stuff I've written, some stuff I've discovered, some stuff I stole." Borrowing is called "nicking" in pop music recording. To "nick" means to be in the groove or to gouge. Sublimely subversive, Dylan always knew that sampling and sharing are ways of transporting and translating material, to renew inspiration and to confound the territoriality of ownership.

(Is copyright mania a refusing of the free-flow of information? Who owns what? The 18th- and 19th-century print-author-editor-copyright mind-frame looks to dam up the sweep and stream of material. Re-establishing borders is a way of reviving direction and authority. Dylan appropriately asked in his 60s anthem, "How does it feel / to be … / with no direction home?" The Copy-Left movement resists the idea of exclusive ownership, confirming the wildfire currents. Planet waves will overflow the banks built by those keen on narrowing the channels.)

"Open a door no man can shut /
and you opened it up so wide."

Deep into his seventies Dylan performed in what he dubbed
The Never Ending Tour, his version of perpetual Exodus. He
crisscrossed the global theatre starting out to perform in large or
small venues following an itinerary he surely shaped from knowing
he must forge ways into the uncreated. He turned his tours into
quests on the road to free his songs from their frames.

Departures are openings that move away from familiar
harbours. At every outset your heart could be light. You've eluded
confinement. Your next gig must be different.

And so, Dylan goes.

He travels from show to show, hypnotizing himself (he said)
to keep burning his being into the musical groove, changing the
keys and tempos of his songs, rarely speaking from the stage,
conceding nothing to his patient loyal audience, the migrant
minstrel with no direction home (what's his true address?) his
nomad identity often unknown to people who meet him on the
street, his destination always the future.

"Au fond de l'Inconnu pour trouver du *nouveau*,"

Charles Baudelaire wrote in "Le Voyage," in his *Les fleurs du mal;* "Il faut être absolument moderne," Arthur Rimbaud announced in *Une saison en enfer.* My translations: "Through the unknown we will find the new;" "You must be absolutely modern..."

Rimbaud read and admired Baudelaire. Conceivably, his incendiary line is a revision of Baudelaire's. Both poets came to their annunciations—Baudelaire in a fit of lyrical anxiety, writing in Paris in the 1850s; Rimbaud in a brazen manifesto-style, writing in the 1870s, likely in Paris—neither knowing (of course) how much more of the new and the modern was to come. Still, each sacrificed himself and his work to developing acute receptivity: they registered sensations—city sprawls, gas-lit boulevards extending the timeline of the night, nervous crowds, telegraph wirings, newspaper-headline uproars, how perception and hallucination collude in the intoxications of drugs and alcohol, streets and masses.

Leonard Cohen was a true heir to the Baudelaire-Rimbaud susceptibility to the pressing of the new. Cohen cultivated a priestly public persona that shrouded his practised seductiveness and his obsession with slippery sex. Although he was seven years older than Dylan, and already admired for his lyrical gift, he followed him into the currents: Cohen knew the times are a-changin', and converted to the accords of radio, stereo, record production and touring after years of writing delicate courtly lines for a sect of devotee readers. The prose in his novel *Beautiful Losers,* his boldest work, flows in the deliberate deliria of the shamanistic beat. Who speaks in its wild pages? You can't be sure. Chants, omens, rituals and orgasms haunt the shadowy speakers in this prose poem. A hermetic work of holy aspiration and erotic dreams, *Beautiful Losers* has its sources in the Book of Ezekiel and Henry Miller's *Tropic of Cancer.* Its depths require patient exegesis.

(Leonard I wrote badly

about you

so-long ago—

I was off—not right

about

what

I said)

A cantor-vagabond, Cohen called himself "a Jewish Buddhist" with Christian affinities. He melded song-writing with a singing style that mixed chanting and reciting. And he needed stillness, he said, finding it in the prayers and meditations of a Zen hermitage. But he could turn interviews into models of diverting cool. And he nurtured Eros by summoning the Renaissance-troubadour traditions of the Languedoc. He cultivated wooing in his voice, pleading and longing in his songs of ravishment and sensual commotion. No one woman would do for him: his audience was his woman, what he ultimately desired. He was the willing slave to these energies.

His *Book of Longing* blended pen-and-ink drawings with graffiti poems that are like found street-koans. His last books were anti-books, refusing finish. Towards the end of his recording and performing time, he started to speak and sing in lower, slower registers—vividly apparent in his last album, *You Want It Darker*. His understanding: to move us into Mystery, he impelled us towards enigmas.

During Cohen's 2012–2013 concerts, after he finished singing his most beloved music to affectionate audiences, he'd kneel bowing his head. His performances seemed to seek grace in inspired new renditions of his songs. He also seemed to be asking for mercy from his listeners and from the Spirit beyond the arenas. His bow acknowledged an end, and devotion. His kneeling seemed a gesture of atonement too, for a transgression or violation he wouldn't, or couldn't, name.

I write believing Cohen listened with his fine inner ear to openings: he could hear sacred and profane tones in the pop amphitheatre. He heard music in its sexual-religious throes, the uncanny heartache.

His gravelled voice had an unmistakable signature in the empathetic networks of poetry and music. "It's closing time, closing time..." he chanted, quoting and echoing Joyce in *Finnegans Wake* and the philosopher Norman O. Brown from his book of the same title. Meaning: here now, quickly one dimension of reality closes, another simultaneously opens.

Cohen grasped how people have always lived on strange thresholds, but our time is flesh-haunted and erotically charged, excessive, devastating, because we vaunt being into the atmosphere (becoming spirit-like ourselves) and we rut in the Earth (looking for grounding in one another's sex). Meditation mandalas and hallelujahs, condoms and strip-teases, eerily inform the tensions of our extremes.

And Patti Smith: her shape-shifting is indelible evidence of a Renaissance sensibility.

She turned her identity search into multiple selves, a refined refusal to settle into one persona. She's been a rock star, a photographer, an installation artist, an archivist, a student of sexual ambiguities and an essayist on Robert Mapplethorpe, Blake, Rimbaud, Jean Genet, Sylvia Plath, Paul Bowles and Sam Shepard. She wrote her name on the waves, becoming its first punk rocker/ slam poet/ memoirist/ eulogist.

Her engagements show how many channels opened in the early 21st century, a Renaissance happening in compressed time.

She once did the unthinkable: she performed the Springsteen song "Because the Night" more authentically than The Boss. Her cover version is the poignant one, "Even better than the real thing…" U2 announced in a song. The U2 line syncs with the preternatural powers of conversion and reinvention available in the pop-whorl.

Curiously, she rarely mentions music in *M Train,* her masterpiece of mourning for the loss of her husband, her brother, her friend and a reassuring world of love. She cites novelists and poets mostly. She makes detailed references to TV shows about detectives and private eyes. Still, her writing exalts a reverent personal space. It's a work of reveries about what she calls "nothing"—the nothing that's truly everything: living passionately, suffering, sudden death, loneliness. Her book is an elegy for the passing of people she loved and a contemplation of quiet nights on the meditative *M Train*, the passage into the Mystery of appearances and disappearances, presence, absence...

She's gifted with the capacity for generosity and friendship. There's truly no one like her in the pop-literary spheres. Simone Weil said, "Generosity and compassion are inseparable." Evolution in hyper-speed has a price. Exacerbated shifts are unbearable for many. Combustions and implosions of identity come in the currents' rages. Openings bring ruptures. Depression, frenzy, addiction, exhaustion and suicide scar the news, afflict the times. The roll call of those who suffered from burnout needs someone who can express mourning and the sweetness of being.

Smith writes absorbing the extremes and transformations of the worldwide cell into passages of muted elegizing and awe. I honour her achievement. *M Train* is a sheltering book. She gives us pages that we read steeped in her kindness, her awareness of the cost and dearness of experience. She has the ability to grieve and bless. In her words I find yearning presence, what it feels like to live with heart.

Then David Bowie. Can we truly say we know who he was? A cunning appropriator of masks and names...

He was born David Jones. He'd call himself Ziggy Stardust, Major Tom, The Man Who Wants to Rule the World, The Thin White Duke, The Man Who Fell to Earth, Blue Genii, Jack Celliers (in the film *Merry Christmas, Mr. Lawrence*), The Elephant Man (a part he once played on Broadway). Masks and more masks. A mask inside a mask...What is the true face? What is behind the appearances?

I call him the unbounded self, the Kabuki poet of multiple-mutable personae of the 70s through to the 2000s. He followed Oscar Wilde's principle that annexing other arts is imperative for ecstasy, the opening of the imagination.

Proudly literary, Bowie produced videos for literacy movements in Canada and the United States, to empower those who couldn't read or write. He'd hold up copies of books by Nietzsche and Dostoyevsky and speak about how they shaped his lyrics. In 1974 William S. Burroughs interviewed Bowie for *Rolling Stone*, the conversation an acknowledgment of apostolic succession, from Beat pastiche writer to a performer who freely plundered sources. Film and stage actor, electronic music experimenter, explorer of recording environments (London, Berlin, Sydney, Montreal, New York), theatrical in his concerts, androgynous sexual sprite and shrewd businessman, he used his ET—extraterrestrial and *Entertainment Tonight*—looks to portray commutable strangeness, creating flash-identities for songs of alienation and the struggle to be human.

A seer of our communications' moment, Bowie understood MTV and how imagery complements and often contradicts words. He understood the magic of quiet, too: he spent ten years "off the record." It wasn't necessary, he said, to be original: just pick up on fads, trends, styles, appearances, machine rhythms, feedback noise, and refine them into your own.

In a way that puzzled observers, he was deeply private. A space-time oddity transcending his cocaine-addled days and his obsession with Aleister Crowley's black magic cult—a dark energy that also attracted Led Zeppelin's Jimmy Page (Page said, "Whether I was attracted to the dark, or it was attracted to me, I don't know...")—Bowie became selflessly devoted to his family and one who required reserved time reading places to feed his need to make new spare work. He understood that the unbounded self becomes dehumanized when you stretch yourself too far. Without gravity the grace of talent may, or will, turn self-destructive.

Yet Bowie retained "a taste for outrage and apocalypse," his friends said. Sensing the alarm and elation, the apogees and abysses of otherworldliness and libertinage that entrance us, he caught songs in styles that oscillated between transcendental yearning and earthly pleasure. In his final video he turned to the biblical story of Lazarus to bravely record his death in public, the crossing over into the ineffable where words and images fail.

His metamorphoses came to an agonized subjectivity. Singing through the mask. Tearing off the mask. The soul breaking through. A ravaged face emerging before the grip of death. His last-will-and-testament video going viral into our spiritual heartland. The mourning time for one this vulnerable in that video and song, and in his strained rasping vocals, was deep and long.

Now we come to a song, a communion moment preserved on a recording...

"We are stardust...

Billion-year old carbon...

We are golden

Caught in the devil's bargain

And we've got to get ourselves

Back to the garden"

These memorable lines come from Joni Mitchell's "Woodstock."

The title yields a feast of meaning. It summons the festival of love and peace that took place on Max Yasgur's farm in upstate New York, August 15th to 18th, 1969. The concert happened 12 km from Woodstock, Dylan's home then, not far from the house called Big Pink where The Band recorded their first epoch-changing LP, beside a town aptly called Bethel. Bethel: the hallowed place in Genesis 28:10-19 where Jacob saw the ladder of angels connecting heaven and Earth.

The music and words to Mitchell's "Woodstock" are available on the web. You can Google them, if you wish.

(Full disclosure: too young to attend Woodstock, I was old enough to hear about it in the news. Then I heard her song and followed her voice into the lyrics' dreamtime.)

She sings of an encounter with "a child of God" at an intersection. Unnamed wanderers... Straying... Together they set off on a trip that leads to a historical turning point...

But her elegiac mood transforms the concert—the fierce sound distortions of Jimi Hendrix, The Who, Sly and the Family Stone, and Ten Years After—into a mythic moment and a song for dreamers and questers. Mitchell: another shape-changer, poet, painter, jazz musician, autobiographical songwriter (in her influential *Blue*), willing to court unpopularity by being experimental.

Her sorrowful voice seems to be performing a kind of penance. What's behind this mysterious tone? The ambiguities thrive.

Her sonic presence is a persona. She was invited to the concert but she didn't attend because she was preparing for an interview with Dick Cavett on his TV show. She intuited the concert's meaning by watching news about it on TV in a New York City motel.

"Woodstock" is a song about soul-making in our cell time of openings, closings: every moment could be a crux, every meeting implies a quest for an authentic life, a greeting is potentially an existential and sacred moment, each path a road towards the point where our imaginations may be "set free," each blessing carries the wound of new awareness, the knowledge that visionary moments pass...

Her song embodies her self-reinventions and the hejira story of the open road. (*Hejira* is the title of one of her best LPs, released in 1976. The word means flight or migration.) Recognizing the presence of revelation in intersections... Strangers meet at a fork in a pathway that could lead to renewal and also to desperation. Loss of identity, pilgrimage, the juncture bringing conversion and the influence of poetry and reveries: they're the crossroads her song creates.

But the dreamtime was brief. The devil's bargain loomed. The Vietnam War informed the brutal backdrop.

We come to a cross-point of appreciation when we truly listen to "Woodstock." The pilgrims from The Canterbury Tales are reincarnated here: so is Rimbaud, who hoboed around France, and so are the New England Transcendentalists, Whitman and Thoreau, and the Beats, Kerouac and Ginsberg, ghostly fellow poets roaming down their odyssey roads. I hear echoes of Dante's

[img22]

steps into the *Commedia* with his guide, Virgil, though these steps go first to Paradise, not to the Inferno. Still, the identities of the singer and the "child of God" are never clearly established. I presume that one—a musician?—is kindly, the other a diviner in the making.

On autobiographical wavelengths, in the aura of associations, the song speaks to Mitchell's border crossings, her changeability. Roberta Joan Anderson changed her name to Joni when she was 13, left Saskatoon, Canada, in the mid-1960s, going to art school in Calgary, then moved to Toronto, where she met and married Chuck Mitchell, an American folksinger. They went to the US, divorcing in the late 60s. By that time she'd already journeyed to California, becoming part of the burgeoning music scene in "the City of Fallen Angels," Los Angeles...

Critics call "Woodstock" a paean to pastoral Utopia, a repudiation of war machines and smog. These readings are true but reductive. Mitchell witnessed the event in the TV beam of images and soundtracks. She recorded her song on a Wurlitzer electric piano, unaccompanied, with few overdubs, in a four-track studio with an analog mixing board. People heard "Woodstock" on the radio and on her *Ladies of the Canyon* LP.

And, again, why is "Woodstock" haunted?

Quests fail...

This is the spell and curse of the open road: open channels can be liberating chasms...

... And the devil's bargain. Something that hasn't disappeared... Waiting to snare us... We know it even if we refuse to name it or try to elude it...

Her song raises the spectre of our contract with malign energy.

How does dark energy grip us? How does it infiltrate the garden, which is the paradise of our senses, the gift of life? We know it in the absence of grace; we know it in the disputing of the value of learning, and in systemic meanness. We feel it in the lack of welcome and absolution between people, in our cynicism over (and fear of) kinship. The devil's bargain comes in the tawdry triumph of materialism and capital over Spirit and imagination. It appears in the suffering of the oppressed and the defrauding of the right to a good life. We know it in the ruthless economics where 1% of the population prospers over everyone else, and where we feel impelled to submit to this merciless inequity. The conditions of the bargain are tragically let loose in the nuclear power we have to wipe life from the Earth, and in the endless attractions of the afflictions of war.

It appears in the venom that's injected into circuits of conversation and dialogue—the poison that causes brutalization, hardening; the harsh tones that seethe into us.

We see the simplistic seductions of dark energy in the separatist aims of nationalist politics and religious extremism. We know it when the Left and the Right turn cruel, adamant, excluding, judgmental, autocratic and dangerously attractive to the unfolding needs and longings of identity. It speaks to the individual soul but consumes the individual spark into the impulsions of fanaticism.

And we know its effects when we experience debilitating fatigue, and the end of trust in the transubstantiating wonders of art. The bargain triumphs when we know that compassion and just relations are best for us, and we'll still do what's for the worst.

Certain energies erupt only when you burn. Openings may bring ferocious forces. This is a troubling reality of suggestible, inspired experience. We can abandon ourselves to possession, dangerous fuels. Immersion can turn into immolation, loss of the self into the fires that kindle from screens.

[img23]

Crosby, Stills, Nash & Young recorded their rock-and-roll version of "Woodstock" for the classic *Déjà Vu*, a return to the event by musicians who were there. Their exuberant take tries to deflect the menacing, twisting energies that distort and taint enthusiasm. This could be the reason why Stephen Stills, a fine singer, sounds breathless, rushing his lyric phrasing so that the words blur. Still, their recording was a pop hit in 1970. CSN&Y creatively misread the lamenting tone of Mitchell's original.

In 1974 she performed a jazz-funk version of "Woodstock," backed up by Tom Scott's LA Express band, on her live double LP *Miles of Aisles*. It's lively, smooth, but swerves off from the eerie way she sang alone in a studio, playing her piano slowly, reflectively.

The original "Woodstock" is her homage to hejiras that reclaim receptive passion. She voyages out to go into "my internal sight," in Milton's words. Call this seering, a new word I've coined to invoke a moment that transfigures physical seeing. Yet the devil's bargain wasn't purged by music and poetry. A recording keeps her song's free sphere.

Her song catches a time that fades in fact and fares forward into the imagination where pilgrims of the spirit meet outside of divisiveness and chronological history. Quests fail, but the Mystery of communion deepens.

And we can recall "Woodstock" anytime on a CD or LP and in the non-locational web where each recalling could be a prelude to asking the questions, "Where do pilgrimages begin? ... Is the vision of harmony a blip? ... Will another crossroads appear? What is the path out of the afflictions of loneliness and despair? How do we stay open to attractions and repulsions without becoming agents of viciousness? What possesses and dispossesses us? ... If we bring hell into our world, then how do we find the beauty in our souls again?"

Dylan, Cohen, Smith, Bowie and Mitchell began their work enthralled by the teenage iconoclast Rimbaud. Prophetically, he said (age 16), "All language being idea… the day of the universal language will come… This language, the *new* or *universal*, will speak from soul to soul, resuming all perfumes, sounds, colours, linking together all thought…"

The five figures shared intuitions about Rimbaud's universal language, the heart's speech. They saw that what he sought in mind-altering drugs and sex, and in the hallucinatory writings called *A Season in Hell* and *Illuminations* (works he never wanted published), had dawned in our ability to be communicants 24/ 7/ 52/ 365 with everyone, and all, via wired and wireless transmissions. We see how Rimbaud's demand that we live in continual crisis through the "immense and reasoned unruliness of the senses" is the new normal (so the viral cliché goes) of the membrane of consciousness and feeling.

Adding:

Van Morrison welcomed the charge when he said, "Too late to stop now," in his song, "Into the Mystic." This ends side one of *Moondance*, his 1970 LP of crises and intimations. He sings in its tracks about how we could embrace alienation and anguish, loneliness and meaninglessness, converting these into what he calls stoning ecstasy (in the LP's first cut) and glad tidings (in its last). "Turn up your radio and let me hear the song / Switch on your electric light / Then we can get down to what's really wrong…" Morrison exults in "Caravan," one of the LP's apogee moments. Nothing curtails the current: it conveys pain, love, consciousness, furies, mutability and light, and caravans on so that we unfold, tracking through our many versions of the wilderness, what we'll perceive and discover for ourselves through the afflictions and joys of our brand-new day, when we flow into the Mystery.

Cusp-artists find ways to live long creative lives by conjuring and configuring the ripple and rush, the wild shifts and darkening divisions. We honour them by following up with our homages, our preservations of complexity and inwardness, our pursuit of wonder, our Eros of creating, our enigmatic cultivations of beauty and spirit, our call and response to those (all of us) who are also empathic pilgrims and know wishing-wells and heartbreak.

It isn't our eyes that need to be wide awake all the time: it's our souls. We can close our eyes but our souls will still long for insight and vision.

Advice to Millennials / Xennials /

Generations X / Y / Z / and Touch /

the Net-gens /

Place your / own cultural references /

here /

Take all the time and space /

you need /

Ecclesiastes' wisdom / says /

each generation must invent /

their touchstones /

and keynotes /

Epigraph 3

"Waves slap on the shore.

And make noises like houses crumbling

many houses falling down..."

"The sea rolls by.

It's like bombs exploding

And when the roll fades away,

The flying sea sings."

From *Miracles: Poems by Children*

[img24]

Introspective aside...

In the time it takes to write revise this, design it, burnish its spaces with images, then publish and publicize it, our conditions will have transfigured again. Transformer Levels (TLs) are at a pitch.

There must be a virtue in being obsolete.

I'm writing trying to find that virtue...

In obsolescence, renewals may come. Trash yards and garbage dumps are sites for found objects and spare parts.

It's been said—by whom?—that it's good to have the avant-garde behind you...

And I have a few more things to say

on

speaking across generations

[img25]

I

To Net-gens and To Whom It May Concern,

    I want to take the chance of writing to you when I know you may never read this. If I had your collective email address I'd use it... But this is what I have... a letter to all or maybe just to one...

    I love writing letters. This one is going over the age gap, one of the distances that can interfere with communion...

    There's a great gulf between us. (And I know I'm speaking to people in developed countries...) Health care, better nutrition, exercise, greater awareness of the effects of smoking and drinking on stamina and depression, have changed life expectancies. In 1900 you might have lived to age 42. In 2018 you could live to 84. In defiance of Nature herself, we may double our age limits again in the next one hundred years. This means the aging population will soon be greater than the young generation (this may have happened already). Marilynne Robinson calls it the experience of "the great graying west," elders looking down on those in their late teens and early twenties, the children of the digital seas who appear rowdy, casual, rewired, irreverent, blurry, attached to tablets and smartphones, endowed with unlimited access to Chromebooks and Androids.

I've met you in classrooms where I talk about books. Many times, I've wondered, what's going on? My colleagues mutter complaints. You're called (brace yourselves), "The generation who can't read... The generation you don't want to care for you when you're old... A pampered generation who must have safe zones in schools to protect them from trigger words... Those on medications because they can't handle stress... Too restless in chairs... So used to texting that telephones are bewildering... A generation so self-involved they'd make Narcissus blink..."

No generation should define the next. You must live in your way.

This is what I see.

It's too easy to condemn what you are. And it's too easy to give in to crankiness over the enigmas you present. I'm following Dylan's advice, "Don't criticize what you don't understand..." The digital seas are your element. Youth is (supposedly) terrific—and sometimes terrifying—for its unconscious ease in the present. And though I sense your anxieties—your vulnerabilities present in the demands you make for your culture to serve you, your confusions over what others ask of you, your unease about what's promised by politicians, your dislike of pre-set conditions (9-to-5 jobs), your mistrust of big institutions—I also sense your place inside the pulsing environment. I'm reflecting on the pulse, observing it, feeling its effects, trying to integrate its processing, in need of quiet and solitude, at home in books and commentaries on them. But you nomads of planetary tides... using fan services and dating sims... scanning on-line fanzines... you stream in the currents...

Do you know the wonder of this? You're fuelling the evolutionary jump-drive... already transnationals, accustomed to cosmopolitanism, all-at-once-ness, using headsets that are spheres of instant entry and alternative takes, improvisational, playful, scattered in thought but capable of seeing many things at once, with X-ray eyes cast on inauthenticity, accepting polymorphous sexuality, rejecting labels, skeptical about theories, intuitive, caught in structures that seem unyielding. I understand you feel bewildered, sometimes patronized, learning and working in places where there are clashes of sensibility, even betrayed by political leaders who are snared in old thought patterns...

People slightly older than you have felt the seductive power of nationalist political movements, the high drama of separatism, and have felt the attractions of extremism and nihilism (the impulse to crash the world down, burn everything up)...

The systems of instruction and economy may now be dead-ends... overworked realities... And you're suffering from their definitions: how elders have set the tone of discussion. High schools and universities, governments and businesses are paralyzed in fear of you, because you're not following paths mapped in advance, demanding more, often asking the sensible questions, "What's alive here... What's true for me?"

(Confession. I was a high school dropout who resisted pre-set patterns because I went looking for life. Though I became a teacher, eventually and uneasily accepting the privileged conditions of a university, I remember shunning the obvious, seeking back-channels of learning to educate myself.)

And because you're vulnerable, skinned to the impulsions of global magnetic fields, our worldwide magnum opus, you must feel naked, easily taken up. Nakedness is the freedom from predictable masks, and nakedness is represented in Blake's painting *Glad Day,* the youthful opening to inspiration (the painting's hue is red).

Your elders may have found wisdom. But many of us have forgotten the lesson of the Book of Job... The whirlwind in one way or another will smash routines, overpower preconceptions.

Look at how #MeToo has suddenly changed us.

The defences of knowledge and ideology are an illusion (for you and me). I know we're often hemmed in by points-of-view that become safe houses, or prisons.

... I take heart realizing that you sense how to live with unpredictability and shape-shifting...

And this is your communications' apogee and abyss...

You come after the ashes of September 11th, 2001... Living in the time when boundaries are disappearing, when there's rampant fear, and city towers with the Trump brand crowd the sky...

Smartphones set to buzz, you're called with vibrations... The Tree of Life now a communications' beacon...

Your locations curved into the atmosphere, your experience one of unending light... cells, PC screens, iCams, night-lamps... sometimes using unfamiliar communicant guides on podcasts and Skype calls, to keep receiving, adapting, scoping, filtering.

And how many of you are born to immigrant families, and carry several passports, and know several languages, comfortably travelling back and forth from Canada to Hong Kong, Morocco, Spain, Iran and India...

And your courage is underestimated: many of you have marched in protests and parades in North America, where such expressions have an honoured if controversial place, but also around the world, in Russia where it's dangerous to dissent...

And you know sex-sites in a way that would have scandalized Anaïs Nin and William S. Burroughs. (I have to use allusions when I talk to you.) Shooting up the sexy *prise de courant*, you go experimenting, feeling the hotwire of flesh, in the moment when the body is experiencing Earth-tremors (chthonic fluctuations) and at the same time your spirit is scooting into the elements. It's erotic liberty meeting the disembodied unmooring...

And this suggests: with Earth energies rising and electronic energies crossing, there are portals that lead to lust and ions meeting, endless titillation. That sounds delirious. But consider how seduction and invitations are part of the Invisible Flux. Its effects felt on skin... YouPorn is the seventh most-accessed site in the world. Number one is the news. Number two... the weather.

And in this way, you embrace humanity's aches. The Great Mysteries at Eleusis began with sex. It's the primary awakening of the senses. Now you can view and involve yourself in lust and longing, horniness and hormones, in the mobile feast, the excess and juice of the orgiastic vastness. You're lightning rods, transmitter-seers too, and the wave forms of energy burn into you and down to your ground, into your roots, in your subconscious, into the Earth, so the fire can move upwards again through your spinal columns into your eyes and ears, into your fingertips... brushing... stroking... sensing... caressing... See what's at your touch... Chemical, biological changes can occur because of cellular influence.

You're called the "Coddled Generation." It's supposed to be a rebuke. It isn't... Intimate with the depths of speed-change, in the beauty and suffering of Gaia, you're inside the supercharged womb of signals and magnetism, in the spin of what engulfs and favours you through earphones, keys, pads and miniaturized screens.

(And when you're moving around and around, channelling so much, your guardian angels must have trouble finding you...)

2

So, what have I learned from you?

You have a kind of co-consciousness, what's called the iBrain, a co-substantiality with the effects of psychic shifts and sensibility changes... It looks like a bearable lightness of becoming and being, though to me it looks difficult because I'm accustomed to cusps and thresholds (living on edge, usually anxious).

Here's a response to your present: you may (or may not) find it helpful.

It's from a book now on my desk. This is what researchers Gigi Vorgan and Gary Small say in *iBrain: Surviving the Technological Alteration of the Modern Mind*:

The current explosion of digital technology not only

is changing the way we live and communicate but

is rapidly and profoundly altering our brains. Daily

exposure to high technology—computers, smart

phones, video games, search engines like Google and

Yahoo—stimulates brain cell alteration and

neurotransmitter release... our brains are evolving

right now—at a speed like never before... not since

Early Man first discovered how to use a tool has the

human brain been so affected so quickly...

Magnetic Resonance Imaging (MRI) indicates the new—
the brain processes information differently when exposed to
select technologies. Summary: books shape one kind of mental
response, electronic devices another. The empirical evidence is
available... (Check it out.) ...You're innocents of a technological
sophistication, your brain waves reshaped by the gadgets you
carry everywhere.

Vorgan and Small again:

The neural networks in the brains of these Digital

Natives differ dramatically from those of Digital

Immigrants... including all baby boomers... who

came to the digital/computer age as adults...

We are witnessing the beginnings of a deeply

divided brain gap...

Paraphrase: what took thousands of years to evolve shifted
in decades (it's worth repeating this).

To apply the Vorgan and Small research: sensitive and
insatiable, responding at high speeds to massive sensory input,
you'll see for yourself how immersion brings techno-brain burnout—
too much adrenalin circuiting into cells and nerves—and the multi-
tasking brain of the cyber-savvy. No wonder you seek guides and
teachers, go on retreats and quests. And no wonder you're soul-
hungry: instead of wisdom you get drug prescriptions for ADD.

(Light, dynamic data-fields, talking into tiny mics, posting images of yourselves, networking, the electrodes of touch, RPM-heat, ultra-sensitivity...

I get it why it's bewildering for you to go to classrooms where books are the ground of learning. Printed letters must seem like hieroglyphs inscribed on a temple wall. It's hard to read because it's an act of exclusionary concentration, focusing on alphabetic configurations for long periods alone in silence. You know digital teeming that mirrors and deepens Creation, the amplitude of images and sounds and the hyper-clicking that keeps you in the loop of communities radiating away from the printed page set before you...)

3

Give me some more moments here. I can't resist going on... writing something... like an essay. Stay with me...

I want to talk about movies. Specifically, terrible ones—Michael Bay's film versions of *Transformers*... Are they essential to you? Not likely... But their images will help us to chart the metaphysics of the media-moment. Yes, they're "Trailer Movies" and "Critic Proof" because they're about relentless motion and sensation. A bad movie—something that isn't *Citizen Kane, The Red Shoes, La Dolce Vita, 2001: A Space Odyssey*—could tell us about what's going on: the frame reveals more than the picture.

I'm sure you'll agree that ours is the great age of CGI magic. There's an exhilarating sophistication to the computer interface with film-making. Digital animation opened movies to vistas, lush worlds of invention. The digital image is unlike the 35-millimetre film-stock image that Charlie Chaplin, John Ford, Orson Welles and Ida Lupino would have used. Sharper, clearer, cleaner, compacted with data, open to morphing and re-editing. Digitized silent and 1930s movies don't look the way they once did (scratchy, fluttery, faded, awkward in their jittering), nor sound like they did (tinny soundtracks with pops and hisses).

But... why *Transformers*...? And which one of the six so far released (should I say blasted at us)? I could include the seemingly endless DC comic superhero movies, from *Batman v Superman* to *Wonder Woman*, to make my point.

Which is...

...they're about transformational shock. They show a metaphysical combat fought above or around human existence and history. These movies capture moments when machine and superpowers and humanity and animal-life collide or fuse...

...In a cosmos of wars breaking out between monsters, masked avengers, hybrid creatures, superheroes, gods and goddesses... the wars render humanity smaller, vulnerable, perplexed, easily trampled on, in dire need of help. History is rewritten, myths rebooted, to show Earth-time is a staged drama— in suburbs, deserts, Chernobyl, Chicago—that obscures the true battles that have raged among divinities and robots. The wars show the Earth and its frail inhabitants to be of enormous importance to other-dimensional creatures, in the (clearly) over-populated cosmos. Something pivotal here I must tell you about... We're animated by sacred and technological energies and diminished by them, in a transcendental wake of high-tech cartoons, CGI spectacles that record a violence and terrorism signalling evolutions to come.

I'm saying the pulp sci-fi fantasy movies show worlds altering more than our thoughts or theories can absorb or articulate. They embody inklings... what we mean when we say the models for human life are cracking, chronological time is an epic story, matter is changeable (mouldable), other ways of being are felt becoming visible, the frontier is being shaped by strange-lings, identity is (again) in freefall...

I'm getting at this your destinies matter

what you are is significant to larger forces

the cosmos is paying attention

the calling of quests continues

Yes, I see how while CGI sophistication grows, plot and character development diminish. Instead of thought-tortured, eloquent Hamlet or dream-obsessed comic Don Quixote (twin figures of Renaissance consciousness and its new humanism), we see inarticulate people in the movies at the behest of gods, aliens, demons, immortal heroes or augmented technologically rewired adepts. (Have you noticed that the superheroes and goddesses speak a neutral, almost mid-Atlantic English, curiously Canadian in its sound? They seldom use contractions or compound sentences.) In Herman Melville's *Moby-Dick*, crazed charismatic Ahab, towering in his Jeremiah-like vision and poetry, hunts the White Whale, symbol of blank inscrutable providence. In *Transformers* and DC superhero movies, the hunted prize is the Earth and humanity.

These movies take for granted the momentum of our hyper-evolutionary jumpstart. They offer insights into the anxiety about radical transfigurations. Every movie ends with a good-evil confrontation, invariably brutal—cities razed, bystanders slaughtered.

And the CGI movies show ESP literacy and technological extension to be natural, a part of how creatures communicate. We find information and insight in gestalts of action, gesture, symbol, image and sound, omissions...

... what's in subliminal backgrounds, between the lines... what's in undercurrents...

Note, a word to the wise guy...

Drugs are (probably!) redundant in the communications' coursing, the sensory tantalizing...

Once, for the poets Coleridge and Baudelaire, drugs broke the conditionings of cliché and custom. Now people use certain drugs to help cope with the evolutionary push, the stress of connective intensities. They're often prescribed to soften the pain of the pressure of too many communiqués. Marijuana, legal in Canada in 2018, is a repose drug, inducing alpha-state reveries... good for listening to music, and helping you to loll...

Our digital-cell environment is a Coke-shot of energy. CGI-IMAX-digital sound-3D movies like stimulants. TV zappers doing the work of LSD... Deep sensitivity and awareness already are a kind of madness. Watch for the blow and the blowback. After the rising comes the crash. And your spirits are angel-wise high, expanding at the white heat, brainwaves and text messages ciphering together...

in the luminous...

vibrations...

4

Okay I'm almost ready to stop. But I want to share an art form I found on the web (free of charge).

In ads for ticket purchases and invitations to meetings, this pops up

No Robots Allowed

Uhhhh?

[An image appears looking like love-struck WALL-E from the Pixar CGI movie]

Please click to confirm you are not a robot

[The icon appears again. You're supposed to admit...]

I am

Human

The ad looks like a script-memo from Ridley Scott´s
Blade Runner...

And it's asking the questions: Are you real? Are you
incarnate? Are you a ghost or a troll? Can you be reached (truly)?

You could be asking me these questions, too.

Let's confirm universal humanity...

Click here.

Advice is only good for passing on. These days it looks like all of us get editorials and lectures instead of prayers and devotions. Still, don't waste your images, don't click away too much of your souls. These are pan-orgasmic conditions and times. Remember that addiction to power is easy. Belonging to a nationalist movement may give temporary purpose and direction, but it will lead to the severing from the struggles of our fellow souls in the commune of longing. And remember, you could pass away unknown on Facebook or Twitter and still be a part of an unparalleled humanity. Blake, Brontë, Dickinson, Rimbaud, Nietzsche and Kafka were mostly unknown in their own time.

...And if you go off the glowing grid, you'll find willow trees and leaves of grass, playful children whispering and laughing behind bushes and hedges. You'll find ripples in creeks mirroring passages of doves, life in perpetual Pentecost speaking to you, the gift waiting for our receptions...

Go in fear of too much irony, which masks cynicism, the urge to deride. Discovering books written by unknowns, and delving into them, is (by the way) a counter-cultural act, a secret route back to quiet and perception. Feel a printed book in your hands; try reading it with earphones and screens turned off. You could be amazed by the quietening and the miracle of letters.

Am I idealizing you? Of course. One of the few things I do well is idealize or romanticize. Why? Because my job is surely to see the ways things could be.

Keep teaching yourselves on or off the grid. Keep teaching us.

I suspect you already know all this.

(Confession again. I wonder if idealism and extremism are twins... Because extremes are also passions... I'm drawn to artists

[img27]

and iconoclasts who go far into revealing and concealing. But what's vital for poets in the independent imagination of creative work looks horrifying when translated into nationalist mania and unhinged Facebook postings.

Then what's light, what's reflection? Becoming in the imagination, its infinite activations... Moments of insurrection and disruption coming from the sparks of originating... Your uprooting into map-less places... Un-selving to re-code, erasing the past... The self its own sublime theatre: so essential for creating. Is all this appalling when consumed by the furies of social media and political extremes?

... could be why I've come to look for a moderate way to live... to remind myself of the humbled path, the light of the everyday...

Another subject, I know...

Thought I'd share it anyway...)

Alone with these pages, my blue-ink pen in hand—yes, I still write by hand—my fingers ink-stained, I reach some quiet and stop for now, look up from my page, and utter welcomes and welcome beginnings.

Yours truly

PS

If I'm wrong about our communications'
moments, then this could be useful. Maybe for
the better... Errors are portals of discovery. Or...
portals are openings that lead to other discover-
ies.

Cycles in history should tell us that the
demand for higher consciousness comes and goes.
Waves turn in time. Think of the Renaissance,
the Romantic period, the beginnings of Modern-
ism, the 1960s. Now we have data-floods and we're
often swept into the current, shaken and carried
along. The waves bring the Mystery, too. We set
out on them.

I'm comforted by a letter William Blake
wrote in 1799 to his exasperated patron the Rev-
erend John Trusler: "I feel very sorry that your
Ideas & Mine... differ so much as to have made
you angry with my method of Study. If I am
wrong, I am in good company..." (I just verified
these lines in a book about Blake. If the book is
wrong... Well.)

I tell myself that even a stopped watch is
right twice a day. (I found this somewhere or
other.)

PPS

Courage and inspirations

always

And here's

Covfefe... to you

so we can share a laugh

Yes, we can hear the beat and feel the beating we're taking...

The global membrane is a heart, its effects like tides in our ears, felt on our skin. Simultaneously, its effects can be a noisy, invasive drive that incites a need to arrest and even kill its pull. Opening time... Closing time... Will one effect prevail over the other? I pray for courageous souls willing to embrace openings and closings. I pray for hearts that can perceive dark energies and dimensions of possibility. I hope for the language of the communion of souls.

We're turning in this whorl, this emergence of planetary consciousness, the time of the galvanized atmosphere of thought and feeling, the impetus and pressures of vast meaning. It's meaning coming to us, from the atmosphere, and a meaning we're projecting, creating with our machines and communicating devices.

Does it matter if any of us like the rapid processes of transformation?

The evolutionary pulse throbs on, in hyper-speed.

A Final Raw Feed (That Isn't So Final)

When your baby comes bawling tiny flesh-red moist fragile and yet bravely there

When the curtains open before the mainframe moment starts

When you see your meal, hot steaming delivered before you in a gleaming dish

When the switches click on the amps before music wings up like a flock of doves in motion

When you see the wave-glitter through the cracks between 50-storey condos that look like Nunataks—an aboriginal word describing mountain guardians that preserve the link between the Earth and sky (more people in cities live high in the air, in buildings that sway in the winds)

When your skin becomes so sensitive you need sunscreen protection every time you open your PC

When getting a charge or getting charged means standing close to a power-bar or a socket or a fuse or a plug and a possession and an empowering and a legacy and the cost (the price you pay) an accusation a conviction and gearing up a sluggish battery (in the winter) and a vitalization getting a chuckle or two ("I get a charge out of that") and going on vacation ("I'm re-charging")

When ECGs (heart monitors) spike from so much stimulation

When our crises, junctures, wounds, covenants, come to decide for us—how we'll evolve—

When we recognize our fear and dislocations

"When the walls come tumbling down"

When our sites startle us away from polarizations and barriers

When in the livestream of thoughts and emotions we sense the other current, the silence beneath behind around inside above the shifts and static—the love beyond the speed of light

When your tongue speaks the light-dark energies with Mystery burning brightly

When we truly rest

When many voices begin to whisper, "Our spirits-souls-imaginations-intuitions-dreams-divinations (our inner lives) are beginning to sync with searches and receptivity, with the need for expansion and breakthroughs, for openness to what's there, to new realities"

When cries and moans become prayers and calls for grace

When your guide is the familiar unfamiliar heartbeat

When in our commune, our homeland of the Spirit, your love your children your friends your partners your co-creators and your once-lost companions are only a moment away, and they write or call through screens or earphones over the air, sending a post that's clichéd but still true

"Greetings /

Blessings /

I hope /

for /

the approach of hope /

sparks /

for / sparks /

of hope /

hope /"

Flash Memos on My Firewall

Homage to Simone Weil

And: the purpose of life—?

More   life

The need of evolution (beyond revolutions) ...?

To end hunger

in its direst form and expression

And: the emphasis of politics?

Give each person space   and time   in the Cosmopolis

Seek just relations

End slavery

Temper force   Reject us versus them

And: culture—art?

Pour out   stories   poetry   Give   voice

Break frames   Speak to loneliness

Access Creation   Be ready for Beauty

Make Cracks for the Source

And: these are lines from Weil's essay "Love of the Order of the World" that sum up what I've been struggling to say about the charge in the global membrane:

Human cities in particular, each one more or less according to its degree of perfection, surround the life of their inhabitants with poetry. They are images and reflections of the city of the world. Actually, the more they have the form of a nation, the more they claim to be countries themselves, the more distorted and soiled they are as images. But to destroy cities, either materially or morally, or to exclude human beings from a city, thrusting them down to the state of social outcasts, this is to sever every bond of poetry and love between human beings and the universe. It is to plunge them forcibly into the horror of ugliness. There can scarcely be a greater crime. We all have a share by our complicity in an almost innumerable quantity of such crimes.

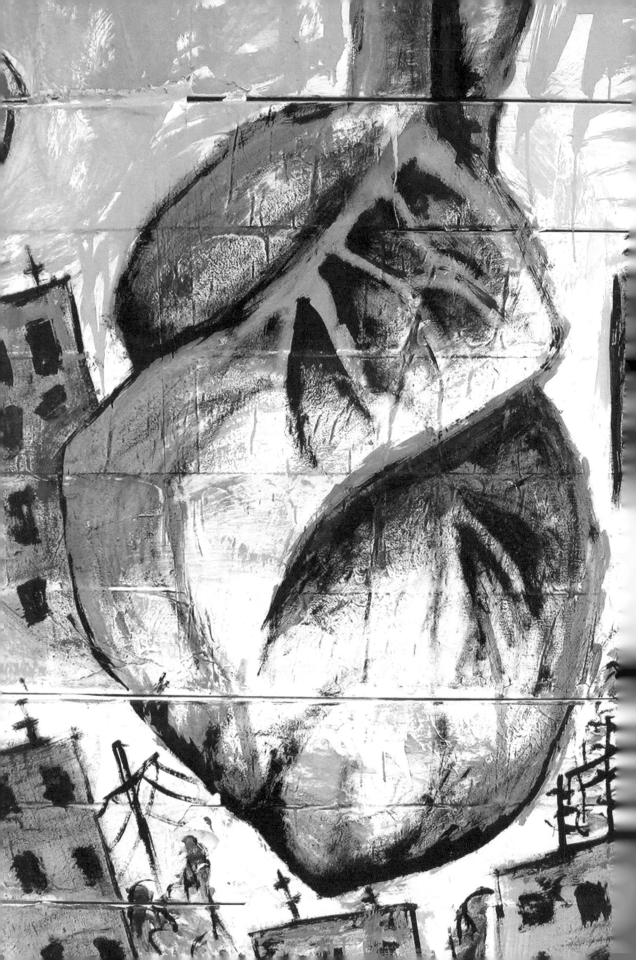

Epigraph 4

"The heart varies from state to state... The lover experiences an [infinite] multifacetedness in the relationship of his love because of the multifacetedness of the Beloved... like the glass chalice, clear and pure, which appears in many different colours, due to different kinds of liquid within it... Only the heart possesses this [constant variability]..."

"My heart has become capable of every form: it is a pasture for gazelles, and a convent for Christian monks, and a temple for idols, and the pilgrim's Ka'ba, and the tables of the Torah and the book of the Quran..."

Ibn 'Arabī, Sufi philosopher (AD 1165-1240)

Here's a blank page

What do you see coming?

Sources

Baudelaire, Charles. *Selected Poems*. Trans. Joanna Richardson. London: Penguin, 1975.

Bedard, Michael. *William Blake: The Gates of Paradise*. Toronto: Tundra, 2006.

Blake, William. *The Marriage of Heaven and Hell*. Oxford: Oxford University Press, 1975.

Bodanis, David. Electric Universe: *How Electricity Switched on the Modern World*. New York: Three Rivers Press, 2005.

Brown, Norman O. *Closing Time*. New York: Vintage, 1974.

Bucke, Richard Maurice. *Cosmic Consciousness: A Study of the Evolution of the Human Mind*. Bedford, MA: Applewood, 2009.

Calasso, Roberto. *Literature and the Gods*. Trans. Tim Parks. New York: Vintage, 2002.

Canetti, Elias. *The Human Province*. Trans. Joachim Neugroschel. New York: Farrar Straus Giroux, 1978.

Carson, Anne. *Float*. Toronto: McClelland & Stewart, 2016.

Cohen, Leonard. *Beautiful Losers*. New York: Viking Press, 1966.

Dickinson, Emily. *Envelope Poems*. New York: New Directions, 2017.

Doidge, Norman. *The Brain that Changes Itself: Stories of Personal Triumph from the Frontiers of Brain Science*. New York: Penguin, 2007.

Dylan, Bob. *Chronicles Volume 1*. New York: Simon & Schuster, 2004.

Emoto, Masaru. *The True Power of Water*. Trans. Noriko Hosoyamada. Hillsboro, OR: Beyond Words Publishing, 2005.

Frye, Northrop. *The Double Vision: Language and Meaning in Religion*. Toronto: University of Toronto Press, 1991.

Ginsberg, Allen. *Your Reason & Blake's System*. Madras, India & New York: Hanuman Books, 1992.

Gopnik, Alison. *The Philosophical Baby: What Children's Minds Tell Us About Truth, Love, and the Meaning of Life*. New York: Farrar, Straus & Giroux, 2009.

Gordon, W. Terrence, with Eri Hamaji and Jacob Albert. *Everyman's Joyce*. New York: Mark Batty, 2009.

Govinda, Lama Anagarika. *The Way of the White Clouds*. London: Rider, 2006.

Gray, Francine du Plessix. *Simone Weil*. New York: Viking, 2001.

Hirtenstein, Stephen. *The Unlimited Mercifier: The Spiritual Life and Thought of Ibn 'Arabī*. Oxford: Anqua Publishing, 1999.

Howe, Susan. *Debths*. New York: New Directions, 2017.

Innis, Harold. "Minerva's Owl." In *The Bias of Communication*. Toronto: University of Toronto Press, 1991.

Lovelock, J.E. *Gaia: A New Look at Life on Earth*. London: Oxford Landmark Science, 1979.

Lewis, Richard (collector). *Miracles: Poems by Children of the English-speaking World*. New York: Simon & Schuster, 1966.

McLuhan, Marshall, and David Carson, with Eric McLuhan and W. Terrence Gordon. *The Book of Probes*. Corte Madera, CA: Gingko Press, 2003.

McLuhan, Marshall, and Eric McLuhan. *Laws of Media: The New Science*. Toronto: University of Toronto Press, 1990.

McLuhan, Marshall, and Harley Parker. *Through the Vanishing Point: Space in Poetry and Painting*. New York: Harper & Row, 1968.

McLuhan, Marshall, with Wilfred Watson. *From Cliché to Archetype*. New York: Harper, 1972.

Paz, Octavio. "Blanco." In *The Poems of Octavio Paz*. Trans. Eliot Weinberger. New York: New Directions, 2012.

Pynchon, Thomas. *Gravity's Rainbow*. New York: Viking, 1973.

Rimbaud, Arthur. *Complete Works*. Trans. Paul Schmidt. New York: HarperCollins, 2008.

Robinson, Marilynne. *The Givenness of Things: Essays*. Toronto: HarperCollins, 2016.

Roob, Alexander. *Alchemy and Mysticism*. Trans. Shaun Whiteside. London: Taschen, 2006.

Rosen, Jonathan. *The Talmud and the Internet: A Journey between Worlds*. New York: Picador, 2000.

Sewell, Elizabeth. *The Orphic Voice: Poetry and Natural History*. New York: Harper & Row, 1971.

Small, Gary, and Gigi Vorgan. *iBrain: Surviving the Technological Alteration of the Modern Mind*. New York: Harper, 2009.

Smith, Patti. *M Train*. New York: Knopf, 2015.

Teilhard de Chardin, Pierre. *The Hymn of the Universe*. Trans. Gerald Vann. New York: Harper & Row, 1965.

—*The Phenomenon of Man*. Trans. Bernard Wall. New York: Harper Torchbooks, 1959.

Wall, Mick. *When Giants Walked the Earth: A Biography of Led Zeppelin*. London: Orion, 2008.

Weil, Simone. *Gravity and Grace*. Trans. Emma Crawford and Mario von der Ruhr. London: Routledge & Kegan Paul, 2002.

—*Waiting for God*. Trans. Emma Craufurd. New York: Harper Perennial, 2009.

—*War and The Iliad*. Essays by Simone Weil, Rachel Bespaloff. Trans. Mary McCarthy. New York: New York Review of Books, 2005.

Yates, Frances A. *The Art of Memory*. Chicago: University of Chicago Press, 1966.

Zukav, Gary. *The Dancing Wu Masters: An Overview of the New Physics*. New York: Bantam, 1989

Artwork

"About the Images: Part of a larger documentary (ethnographic) project, the images of street art were photographed as they were found in various cities on particular days. Often, they are the result of collective creativity illustrating the Charge in the streets, and credit for their creation remains with the original artists. I hope these images will provide wider exposure to artists and allow them to spread their news and views."

Marshall Soules

Acknowledgments

I'm grateful to the following people and works who helped during the writing of this book: Maria Auxiliadora Sanchéz Ledesma, Dale Winslow, Alex Kuskis, W. Terrence Gordon, Cristina Miranda de Almeida, Matteo Ciastellardi, Barbie Halaby, Mauro Buccheri, Jason Buccheri, Karl Leschinsky, Lindsay Presswell, Jerry Harp, Corinne and Eric McLuhan (a special thanks to Eric), Patricia Keeney, Oliver Kruger and his essay "Gaia, God, and the Internet" (which I read after writing my last version of this work), Diane Keating, Raven and David Murphy, Elaine Kahn, Jim Berry, Wilfred Cude, J.S. Porter, Elias Canetti, James Hillman, Octavio Paz's "Blanco," Charlene Jones who helped me to articulate Gaia and #MeToo, Bob Dylan's "Visions of Johanna," Sylvia Plath's "Lady Lazarus," Ridley Scott's *Blade Runner*, Susan Howe, Lance Strate, Paolo Granata, Friederike Bental, Katie Powe, Tom Powe, Jeremy Earley, Kathleen Powe, Marta Garcia, Anna Veprinska, Gavin Currie, Ivona Jozinovic, Chris Durand, Margaret Lee, Kathy Tsukalas, my students in English 4004 and 4163 in 2016, 2017 and 2018 at York University in Toronto, and all at IN3 at the University of Catalunya in Barcelona from 2011 to 2015.

I adapted the phrase "writing and reading in freefall" from Anne Carson's *Float*. And I acknowledge controversies surrounding Simone Weil's pronouncements on Judaism and Christianity. I'm not in agreement with her, in these. Judaism and Christianity for me aren't irreconcilable; they're brethren, one born out of the other. Still, I'm fascinated by her theological urgency. I revere her indispensable mix of "mysticism and social activism," in the vivid words of her biographer, Francine du Plessix Gray.

Homages, translations, quotations, paraphrases, samplings, revisions, misread passages, imitations, assumed statements, overheard or misheard remarks have migrated into these pages in one way or another during the period of its writing, from March 2017 through June 2018. An embryonic version of it was published on-line through the McLuhan Network by Alex Kuskis in May 2017. I'm deeply indebted to everyone at NeoPoiesis Press who designed the pages, and to my friend and co-creator, Marshall Soules, who commented on the writing and envisioned the brilliant counterpoint of images.

Biographical Notes

B.W. Powe is a writer and a teacher. He has written over 14 books of poetry and prose, and he teaches at York University. He lives in Canada and Spain.

Marshall Soules is the former Chair of Media Studies at Vancouver Island University and author of *Media, Persuasion and Propaganda* (2015) among other works. He has been photographing wall art since the 1980s.

CPSIA information can be obtained
at www.ICGtesting.com
Printed in the USA
LVHW072244160419
614446LV00027B/666/P